BELIEVERS, THINKERS,

AND

FOUNDERS

BELIEVERS, THINKERS,

AND

FOUNDERS

HOW WE CAME TO BE
ONE NATION UNDER GOD

KEVIN SEAMUS HASSON

IMAGE

NEW YORK

Copyright © 2016 by Kevin Seamus Hasson

All rights reserved.
Published in the United States by Image,
an imprint of the Crown Publishing Group,
a division of Penguin Random House LLC, New York.
www.crownpublishing.com

IMAGE is a registered trademark and the "I" colophon
is a trademark of Penguin Random House LLC.

Library of Congress Cataloging-in-Publication
Data is available upon request.

ISBN 978-0-307-71818-1
eBook ISBN 978-0-307-71820-4

Printed in the United States of America

Jacket design by Jessie Sayward Bright

2 4 6 8 10 9 7 5 3 1

First Edition

FOR MARY

CONTENTS

Contents

ACKNOWLEDGMENTS

I 'm greatly indebted to many people who have made possible completing this book, while I continue to battle Parkinson's disease. In a category by herself is my wife, Mary Rice Hasson, who has not only made the book possible but, at considerable personal sacrifice, has made life livable. I'm grateful to family and friends—to my daughter, Mary C. Goe, who is a fantastic research assistant; to Mitch Boersma, Lori Windham, and Scott Walter, who each drafted portions of the book; to Bill Mumma and Kristina Arriaga de Bucholtz and all my colleagues, past and present, at the Becket Fund for Religious Liberty. I'm particularly indebted to the Becket Fund lawyers who worked on our legal briefs in the early Pledge of Allegiance cases: Derek L. Gaubatz, Luke Goodrich, Jared Leland, Anthony R. Picarello, Jr., Eric Rassbach, Roman P. Storzer, and Diana Verm. Some of the material appearing in this book is taken from those briefs.*

Other material appeared previously in my articles "Religious Liberty and Human Dignity: A Tale of Two Declarations," *Harvard Journal of Law & Public Policy* 27 (September 22, 2003), and "The Myth: Is There Religious Liberty in America?" *American Spectator* (February 2008).

---

* *Elk Grove Unified School District v. Newdow,* No. 02-1624 (USSC filed December 19, 2003), Brief Amicus Curiae of the Knights of Columbus; *Newdow v. Rio Linda Union School District,* No. 05-17257 (9th Cir. filed June 1, 2006), Opening Brief of Defendant-Intervenor-Appellants; *Newdow v. Rio Linda Union School District,* No. 05-17257 (9th Cir. filed Sept. 5, 2006), Reply Brief of Defendant-Intervenor-Appellants; *Freedom from Religion Foundation v. Hanover School District,* No. 09-2473 (1st Cir. filed April 7, 2010), Response Brief of Defendants-Appellees; *Doe v. Acton-Boxborough Regional School District,* No. SJC-11317 (Mass. Feb. 11, 2013) Response Brief of Defendant-Intervener-Appellees; *American Humanist Association v. Matawan-Aberdeen Regional School District,* No. 1317-14 (N.J. Super. Ct. Law Div. filed Oct. 7, 2014), Motion to Dismiss of Defendant-Intervenors; *American Humanist Association v. Matawan-Aberdeen Regional School District,* No. 1317-14 (N.J. Super. Ct. Law Div. filed Nov. 13, 2014), Reply in support of Motion to Dismiss of Defendant Intervenors.

It is used here with the kind permission of the respective journals.

I'm very grateful to Dr. Theresa Farnan, to my eldest son Mike Hasson, to Andrew Zwerneman, and to Jeannette DeCelles-Zwerneman, who all read the manuscript and suggested improvements. Errors that remain are due to my stubbornness.

Finally, I'm very grateful to Gary Jansen, senior editor at Penguin Random House, and Amanda O'Connor, associate editor, for their extraordinary patience and kindness.

PART

I

Newdow's Conundrum

How can they get away with it? Public school-teachers couldn't lead their classes in pledging allegiance to "one nation under Jesus," could they? So how can they get away with "one nation under God"?

That was the essence of atheist-activist Michael Newdow's famous challenge to the words *under God* in the Pledge of Allegiance as he was representing himself before the Supreme Court of the United States.[1] He was adamant about it. When asked by Justice Stephen Breyer, what if the phrase *under God* were read very broadly, almost symbolically, Newdow said it wouldn't

BELIEVERS, THINKERS, AND FOUNDERS

matter: "I don't think that I can [read] 'under God' to mean 'no God,' which is exactly what I think."[2] And if the meaning of the phrase *under God* couldn't be stretched as far as dogmatic atheism, then it wasn't nearly elastic enough to be constitutional in Newdow's book. So, no "one nation under Jesus," no "one nation under God." Period.

It was an extraordinary moment, even by Supreme Court standards. Here was a litigant claiming the *constitutional* right to forbid public schoolchildren from invoking the traditional source of all of their, and our, *natural* rights. What's more, his argument had a certain logic to it, albeit in an appalling sort of way. If you couldn't say "one nation under Jesus," just how could you say "one nation under God"? Call it Newdow's Conundrum.

America's traditional theory of rights is an elegant one: the government must respect our rights because they come to us from a source prior to, and higher than, it. Compare our theory of rights to that of Magna Carta. Signed at Runnymede by King John of England in 1215, Magna Carta was a landmark document drafted by feudal barons to limit the king's powers. Magna Carta states, in part, that "we grant to God . . . that the English church is to be free and to have all of its rights fully and its liberties entirely." "Grant to God." Hilarious. In Magna Carta, the king actually purports to grant rights to God.

By contrast, the Declaration of Independence insists that rights enforceable against the king are given by God to each individual. As the Declaration puts it, our rights are "endowed" to us by no one less than the "Creator" himself, so no merely human power may legitimately deprive us of them. If all goes well, the state can and should *secure* our rights in law—"secure the blessings of liberty" as the preamble to the Constitution says. If things go wrong, the state can, and too often does, *violate* our rights. But that's the worst it can do. It can't actually amend or nullify the rights themselves. They didn't come from the state in the first place, so the state can't take them away. They come from the "Creator," which is why they're "inalienable," so the theory goes. In the tradition of James Madison and Thomas Jefferson, we are a nation "with liberty and justice for all" because we are a "nation under God."

Michael Newdow, though, begged to differ. He wanted his daughter and all public school-children to pledge their allegiance only to a very different sort of nation. That nation, as envisioned by Newdow, would also offer liberty and justice for all—but it could do so *only* because it would *not* be "under God." Otherwise, in his view, it wouldn't be offering liberty and justice for atheists. The secularist challenge to the American tradition had thus finally reached its logical extreme—America: One Nation Under Nobody.

Popular outrage continued to erupt. Ever since a lower court, the U.S. Court of Appeals for the Ninth Circuit, in San Francisco, had struck down *under God* in the case almost two years before, an assortment of voices had vied with one another to see who could pour the most scorn on that court's opinion. The bases for the criticisms varied widely. And some were more coherent than others.

The most strident gave short shrift to Newdow's Conundrum. In fact, they flatly denied its premise. To hear them tell it, America was, always had been, and must always be a formally Christian country. For them, the term *under God* in the Pledge, like the terms *Creator* and *Nature's God* in the Declaration of Independence before it, could properly be understood only as shorthand for the Blessed Trinity. Only the Living God was potent enough to truly endow us with rights. And as Christians, they firmly believed that the Living God had revealed Himself as Father, Son, and Holy Spirit. So what else could the Declaration and Pledge possibly mean? They concluded it was absolutely essential to have public schoolkids begin their schooldays invoking the Blessed Trinity. And if being able to pledge allegiance to "one nation under Jesus" was what it would take to ensure that, well then, so be it.

Watching this spectacle play itself out, many

observers groaned almost in chorus, "Here we go again." It's understandable. We've long become numb to annual fights over nativity scenes and menorahs. And we barely even notice the now-year-round arguments over public school plays, Halloween parties, Easter egg hunts, and so forth. So when confronted with yet another installment in a seemingly endless saga, we tend simply to roll our eyes, change the channel, and do our best to ignore it.

But this one is different. The fight over the Pledge of Allegiance isolates the essential legal and philosophical debate of the culture war and then takes it to its logical extreme. It sets up a supposed dilemma that pits our constitutional rights against the underlying idea of natural rights in the first place. So despite the all-too-familiar cast reprising their well-worn lines, this episode really is worth watching. This time a great deal is at stake.

OF PILGRIMS AND PARK RANGERS

The players certainly are familiar. In fact, we've seen them over and over again. Broadly speaking, the day-in, day-out dramas over religion in public culture feature the extras of two troupes of veteran ideologues. One persuasion, which I dubbed the "Pilgrims" in my previous book, *The Right to Be Wrong,* are like the fine but fundamentally confused folk of Plymouth Colony, who would permit only their own faith to be practiced publicly. Modern-day Pilgrims, like their namesakes, undervalue the inherent dignity of even a mistaken conscience, and so they continue to insist that only their true faith belongs in public life.

Pilgrims can be found in many faith traditions. Some are dangerous, would-be-shoe-bomber types who must be opposed at all costs. The vast majority, however, are very far from it. Nevertheless, their blundering about can still cause real harm. They make the same big

BELIEVERS, THINKERS, AND FOUNDERS

conceptual mistake as do their more hard-core colleagues: they think the truths they hold trump other people's freedom.

The opposing ideologues, the "Park Rangers" in *The Right to Be Wrong,* are named after the hapless bureaucrats in a too-good-to-be-true story set in Golden Gate Park in San Francisco. The Japanese Tea Garden in the park has, for many years, been a delicately groomed and widely beloved refuge from some of the grittier aspects of urban life. One day in 1989, however, that changed. One of the park workers had jettisoned a surplus parking barrier at the back of the Tea Garden, and the bullet-shaped lump of granite had begun to disrupt the visual harmony of the place. For roughly four years, the local bureaucrats (the "Park Rangers") had resisted all calls to remove the stone plug—until a small band of New Agers, who had stumbled upon it, pronounced the parking barrier a manifestation of the Hindu god Shiva and began to worship it. Whereupon the Park Rangers roused themselves and swung into action, announcing that it was their duty to put a stop to worship on (and in this case, of) public property. The New Agers promptly sued for the return of their deity, and the case quickly settled. The Park Rangers handed over the surplus parking barrier to its devotees who, for their part, agreed to worship it in private, someplace else. The moral of the story? For Park Rangers, truth claims about God—no matter how harmless— have no place in public culture.

Most Park Rangers are well intentioned, if misguided, and are not exactly the intrepid culture-warrior type. In fact, like their namesakes in San Francisco, they more closely resemble the Keystone Kops than the Thought Police. Most Park Rangers act not out of a considered ideological commitment so much as a vague assumption that this is somehow their civic duty. They are each doing their bit, as they see it, to keep the Pilgrims at bay. These sorts of garden-variety Park Rangers can still do real damage to the culture. Nevertheless, like the run-of-the-mill Pilgrims, they tend to be more a nuisance than a menace.

Some Park Rangers, though, really are hard-core ideologues who are utterly convinced that we humans must face the facts. We are, they say, nothing more than accidental organisms adrift in a cold and lonely universe, no more inherently noble than any other carbon compound. For them, any instinct we feel toward transcendence is really just a cruel, Freudian joke that we ought consciously to confront and resolutely reject. They think human flourishing is best served by banishing temptations to believe in God that ultimately only worsen people's angst. The Pledge of Allegiance's assertion that we are "one nation under God" is their Exhibit A. They will not budge: transcendent truth-claims, no matter how attenuated, simply cannot be allowed out in public, certainly not in public schools. In short, where Pilgrims hold that the truth trumps other people's freedom, the Park Rangers hold the polar opposite: their freedom trumps other people's truth.

Each extreme is problematic. Newdow's and his fellow Park Rangers' theory ends up making rights nothing more than gifts from the government. And government gifts are always liable to be revoked. What the government gives, the government can take away. Under the Pilgrims' "Christian country" theory, we would have the opposite problem. True, our rights might be more firmly grounded, but what sort of rights would they be? If the government could require people to profess a certain faith, what couldn't it decree? Each extreme brings with it its own particular risk.

This conflict, however, is even more perilous than it first seems. If the Park Rangers were to win, it would do great harm not only to the culture, but to our theory of rights. And so, of course, would a (highly improbable) win by the Pilgrims trying to establish America as a formally Christian country. What is less apparent is the damage that would result if the Pledge's "under God" language were to be upheld on a mistaken rationale.

STANDING ON CEREMONY

I n *Murder in the Cathedral,* T. S. Eliot portrays Thomas Becket as he faces the prospect of martyrdom by the knights of Henry II. Becket's final temptation is to embrace martyrdom for the sake of his own glory. He responds to the tempter:

> *The last temptation is the greatest treason:*
> *To do the right deed for the wrong reason.*[3]

Those who would defend keeping *under God* in the Pledge of Allegiance, maintaining the national motto, and the like, face a similar bedevilment. There is a strong temptation for government officials, pundits, lawyers, and even some judges and Justices to defend such things as the Pledge by deploying a nobody-in-here-but-us-secular-sophisticates defense. That's an argument that says, in essence, "Not to worry. Saying 'one nation under God' is like saying 'God bless you' when somebody sneezes—it's a meaningless formality. It's not worth getting upset about." The *New York Times,* in its editorial on the Newdow case, opined that *under God* was inserted into the Pledge in what it called "an absurd attempt to link patriotism with religious piety at the height of anti-Communist mania [that] should never have happened." Not to worry though. The *Times* assured us that "in the half-century since, the phrase has become part of the backdrop of life."[4] Move along now. Nothing to see here; just some schoolkids mindlessly mumbling something they've memorized.

Those who wish to make this argument usually seize on a rather confused notion known as "ceremonial deism." No philosopher or theologian—and certainly no Deist—had ever imagined such a term. It originated with Dean Eugene Rostow, of Yale Law School, in a 1962 lecture.[5] No Supreme Court Justice picked up on it for over twenty years, until Justice William J. Brennan invoked it in his 1984 dissent in *Lynch v. Donnelly,*[6] a case in which a sharply divided Court permitted Pawtucket, Rhode Island, to continue including a nativity scene in its public Christmas display. Justice Brennan didn't think the nativity scene was constitutional, but in his dissenting opinion he mused that some references to the divine in our public life might be tolerable:

> I would suggest that such practices as the designation of "In God We Trust" as our national motto, or the references to God contained in the Pledge of Allegiance to the flag can best be understood, in Dean Rostow's apt phrase, as a form of *"ceremonial deism,"* protected from Establishment Clause scrutiny chiefly because they have lost through rote repetition any significant religious content.[7]

Five years later the phrase turned up in an even more badly splintered Supreme Court case, *County of Allegheny v. ACLU.*[8] There, shifting majorities on the Court ended up deciding that a nativity scene had to go but a menorah could stay.

The last time any member of the Court seriously advanced ceremonial deism was in a 2004 concurring opinion written by (now retired) Justice Sandra Day O'Connor in Newdow's case itself.[9] There, she wrote that she would have upheld "under God" in the Pledge, essentially because everybody knows we don't really mean it anymore.

In short, ceremonial deism is a mess. "Winning" a Pledge case on that basis would be almost as bad as losing. The specific practice at issue might be allowed to continue, but the condition under which it would continue would set a precedent that in short order would poison our theory of rights.

Is there no solution, then, to Newdow's Conundrum? Can we really maintain a principled, robust reading of the First Amendment only at the cost of emasculating the basis of natural rights in the first place?

Well, what if neither horn of the dilemma is quite as pointed as it seems? What if it is possible to ground our rights, as the Declaration does, firmly in our "Creator," while scrupulously defending the rights of dissenters, and without sliding down the slippery slope toward theocracy?

Put differently, what if it is possible for the government to acknowledge the existence of a God who is the source of our rights—and mean it— without doing so religiously? What if, at least sometimes, the existence of God is a philosophical conclusion and not a religious dogma at all?

No doubt, to many, even asking those questions will seem almost laughable. How could anything about *God* ever not be *religious*? As we'll see, however, rationally asking whether God exists is a perfectly respectable thing to do. In fact, whether it's reasonable to conclude that there's a Supreme Being is a question that's been debated for millennia, entirely apart from any religious teachings. The question of God's existence has provoked lively *philosophical* debate ever since Aristotle. And it's not just a discussion among academics but a question that's been implicitly asked and answered by legions of ordinary Somethingists along the way ("I don't believe in any religion, but I'm sure Something is out there"). Moreover, what if such knowledge of God—call him (with apologies to Pascal) the

"Philosophers' God"—were precisely what the Founders had in mind when they wrote the Declaration and the other documents standing in that tradition? What then?

Those questions are the subject of this book. We'll first explore the inadequacies of both the Pilgrim and the Park Ranger models. (In order to appreciate fully the solution, we must be duly appalled at the scope of the problem.) We'll begin with the sad but heroic stories of a handful of schoolchildren and their parents who stood tall for their rights when all around them, loud voices—including those of the courts—were attempting to shout them down. Theirs were the first two Pledge cases to reach the Supreme Court, decades before Michael Newdow's.

CHAPTER TWO

The Pilgrims Pledge Their Allegiance . . .

Michael Newdow wasn't the first person to challenge the Pledge of Allegiance before the Supreme Court. Two generations earlier, Lillian Gobitis and Marie Barnette brought their own challenges, several years apart. Their distressing stories illustrate well the value of a robust First Amendment. They show us why it is a good thing to take seriously even children's rights to free speech and the free exercise of religion. And they remind us of what can happen when Pilgrims are in charge.

LITTLE ONES STANDING TALL

The Barnette and Gobitis families were 1930s-era Jehovah's Witnesses who had come to believe that saluting the flag was equivalent to idol worship, and so refused to do it.[1] Now this was the Pledge of Allegiance before Congress amended it in 1954 to include the phrase *under God*. (We'll return to that story later.) So what was involved here was not a claim that the government was pushing an officially favored religion on the Jehovah's Witnesses. Rather, the complaint was that the government was preventing them from freely exercising their own officially *dis*favored religion and from exercising their freedom of speech. As we'll see, that distinction between pushing religious exercise and preventing religious exercise is an important one.

In the early 1930s, Jehovah's Witnesses weren't exactly everyone's favorite citizens. Often direct and sometimes abrasive, they were notorious for their confrontational recruiting tactics. What's more, as committed conscientious objectors, they refused to bear arms in support of the United States.

(Many went on to sacrifice their lives in noncombatant service, but that's another book.) Then in 1935, church leaders announced that church members should not join in flag salutes because such things were idolatrous. The already unpopular faith became even more suspect.

For eleven-year-old Lillian Gobitis and her ten-year-old little brother, Billy, that meant that, in conscience, they had to stop saluting the flag in school—something that didn't go over well in tiny Minersville, Pennsylvania. Lillian, once popular, had to give up her position as class president. Billy's teacher physically tried to wrest his hand from his pocket when the class stood to salute the flag.[2]

The school board didn't know what to do with the Gobitis children. There was no law that permitted punishing children for refusing to say the Pledge, so they asked state education officials for authority to enact one. The state agreed, and at the next board meeting they promptly established a policy of expelling children who refused to say the Pledge.

The Gobitis family had made their case to the school board. And Billy had written a letter that explained, "I do not salute the flag not because I do not love my country but I love my country and I love God more and I must obey his commandments."[3] Nevertheless, the board passed the policy and then immediately held a second vote, this time voting to expel Lillian and Billy from school, without appeal.[4] Their already-struggling parents, owners of the local grocery, had to transform their delivery truck into a makeshift school bus to drive them and other local children to a Jehovah's Witness school in another town.[5]

FIRST AMENDMENT, TAKE ONE

E ventually they sued, arguing that the school board's policy violated their First Amendment rights to freedom of speech and the free exercise of religion. The district court in Philadelphia agreed with them—it ruled that refusal to say the Pledge was a part of their First Amendment rights. The school district immediately appealed. But the Court of Appeals for the Third Circuit agreed with the Gobitis family, too. So the school district took its case for forcing Lillian and Billy to violate their consciences to the Supreme Court of the United States.

There, things were different. The Supreme Court heard the case in April 1940, as Germany was invading Norway. Europe was plunging into war, and American involvement looked inevitable. Hardly a politically astute moment to refuse to pledge allegiance. Less than six weeks later, as the Germans marched through France, the Supreme Court handed down an 8–1 opinion saying the Gobitis children had no right to refuse to say the Pledge of Allegiance. The Court believed that patriotism and national unity were paramount. "A society . . . may in self-protection utilize the educational process for inculcating those almost unconscious feelings which bind men together in a comprehending loyalty, whatever may be their lesser differences and difficulties," it said.[6] And that was that.

Reaction to the *Gobitis* opinion was swift and ugly. Already unpopular, Jehovah's Witnesses were now labeled outright traitors. It was widely believed that the rapid fall of France had been due to a fifth column of Nazi sleeper agents, and paranoia about a similar attempt in the United States ran high. Because of the Jehovah's Witnesses' refusal to bear arms or to salute the flag, many accused them of being Nazi sympathizers or even the dreaded fifth column itself. (Later we would learn that Jehovah's Witnesses in Germany were being sent to concentration camps for their refusal to salute Hitler.)[7] In Odessa, Texas, Jehovah's Witnesses were rounded up and marched out of town, physically carrying some of their weaker members after several collapsed from heat exhaustion.[8] In Kennebunk, Maine, a crowd stormed into a Kingdom Hall and set it on fire.[9] When the flames went out, the crowd relit them. Then they piled the Witnesses' possessions on the front lawn and burned those for good measure. In Wyoming, a Jehovah's Witness was tarred and feathered.

This was systematic, legal persecution of a small religious minority. In West Virginia, the state passed a law quoting the *Gobitis* decision and requiring schoolchildren to say the Pledge.[10] In one town, a group of Jehovah's Witnesses were roped together, forced to drink castor oil, then marched through town in an attempt to humiliate them into submission.[11]

So it was all the more heroic that two West Virginia schoolchildren, ten-year-old Gathie and eight-year-old Marie Barnette, were still refusing to say the Pledge at Slip Hill Grade School outside Charleston. Like the Gobitis children, the Barnettes were Jehovah's Witnesses, and also like the Gobitis children, they believed that to salute the flag was tantamount to idol worship. The school sent the girls home for refusing to say the Pledge, but it couldn't force them to comply. Local authorities threatened to fine or even imprison their parents for keeping the girls out of school. So every morning Marie and Gathie walked to the schoolhouse, sat down in class, remained seated for the Pledge, and were promptly sent home. "It was fortunate we lived fairly close—we didn't have a long distance to go," Marie would recall years later.[12]

Meanwhile the Supreme Court was following the aftermath of its decision with growing dismay. Three Justices who had signed on to *Gobitis* wrote an opinion in an unrelated case saying they had made a mistake.[13] And President Roosevelt appointed a new Justice to the Supreme Court, Robert H. Jackson, who had already criticized *Gobitis*. Together with Justice Harlan F. Stone, the lone dissenter in *Gobitis,* and the three other justices who had changed their minds, that made five. The Court now had the votes to overrule *Gobitis*. For the first time since the original decision, things were looking up for Jehovah's Witnesses.

First Amendment, Take Two

So they tried again. The Barnette family brought suit in federal court on behalf of their girls and other Jehovah's Witnesses who refused to say the Pledge. And at the district court, against all odds—they actually won. The district court did the math and realized that a majority of the Supreme Court Justices wanted to overturn *Gobitis,* so it granted an injunction in favor of the Barnettes.

Outraged, the state appealed directly to the Supreme Court. Now, for the Jehovah's Witnesses, the atmospherics really hadn't improved at all. True, America was no longer rushing headlong into war. Instead, it had actually been waging war for eighteen months, with casualties mounting and no end in sight. Pearl Harbor was still fresh on the nation's mind, and two groups of Nazis had recently been arrested after landing on beaches in New York and Florida and were sentenced to death for planning attacks on American soil.[14] The dangers were real, the threats were immediate, and few wanted to stand beside people who refused to pledge allegiance to their country.

But the dangers to religious freedom were now more apparent, too. The Supreme Court was

aware of the violence carried out against Jehovah's Witnesses, and many believe this was the
reason for the public repudiation of the *Gobitis*
opinion.[15] In any event, when the issue arrived at
the Supreme Court for the second time, it found
the Court ready to rebalance national unity with
respect for religious freedom.

The case was argued in March 1943, and
three months later the Supreme Court issued
what would become one of its best-known opinions, holding that the government did not have
the power to forcibly impose the Pledge on anyone: "If there is any fixed star in our constitutional constellation, it is that no official, high or
petty, can prescribe what shall be orthodox in
politics, nationalism, religion, or other matters of
opinion or force citizens to confess by word or
act their faith therein."[16]

GETTING THE RIGHT RIGHT

Just as remarkable as what the Supreme Court did is what it didn't do. Relying upon the Free Speech and Free Exercise Clauses of the First Amendment, it didn't throw out the Pledge altogether. It didn't ban it from public schools, or prohibit teachers from leading the Pledge's recitation. Instead, it protected the Barnettes' right to opt out, while allowing the rest of their classmates to continue saying the Pledge voluntarily. Live and let live.

The *Barnette* approach is significantly different from the approach the Court has taken in Establishment Clause cases. That clause, when read through the lens of the Fourteenth Amendment, has been held to forbid states, among other things, from promulgating official prayers. In subsequent school prayer and Bible-reading cases, for example, the Court did not provide an opt-out, the way it had for the Barnette children. Instead, it halted the prayers and the Bible-reading exercises completely.

What's the difference? Why allow the school recitation of the Pledge to remain intact, then ban the so-called Romper Room Prayer ("God is great. God is good. Let us thank Him for our food?") over far more abstract objections?

The difference is the nature of the constitutional right that is at issue in each case. In the school prayer cases, for example, the state was held to be in violation of the First Amendment's Establishment Clause. So as harmless as the Romper Room Prayer may have sounded, it is indeed a *prayer*. And leading prayer was something the Court had held the government may never do. It followed that, when presented with a lawsuit challenging that practice in a public school, the Court could properly order it halted completely.

In the *Barnette* case, by contrast, the Court was faced with a different sort of claim. By leading schoolchildren in the Pledge, the government was not making any sort of religious assertion at all; it was making a variety of patriotic and philosophical ones. Under the Free Speech and Free Exercise Clauses of the First Amendment, the government could not force the Barnette children to express those sentiments against their consciences. But leading other willing children in the Pledge violated nothing in the Constitution.

In short, the Free Speech Clause and the Free Exercise Clause protect dissenters from having to convey a government message they don't believe. Those clauses do not, however, prevent the government from speaking that message itself. But if the message is a quintessentially religious one—like the Romper Room Prayer—that violates the Establishment Clause, it is not enough simply to give dissenters an opt-out. The nature of the offense requires that the government itself must be silenced.

(This distinction between the legal treatment of government theological statements on the one hand, and government philosophical statements on the other, is one we'll return to later. Hold that thought.)

But why is it important that the government be able to make philosophical assertions at all? If people can dissent from them anyway, why bother? Because it's important that the government acknowledge the ultimate source of our rights and thus the limits of its powers. That's a larger issue we'll return to later.

Meanwhile, it also bears emphasis that one particularly important such limit is the right of the people to dissent. And that right is especially difficult for the state to respect. It is a right extending even to those like Michael Newdow who deny the traditional account of the source of their—and our—rights. (Of course, the fact that a strong majority of Americans agrees with the traditional account helps keep the government on a short leash. British writer G. K. Chesterton once quipped, "Thank God there are pacifists, and thank God there aren't more of them." Perhaps something similar may be said of dissenters like Newdow.)

It is both painful and embarrassing to read the stories of petty government bureaucrats administering everything from castor oil to tar and feathers to American citizens who simply wished to obey their consciences and not pledge their allegiance to something their faith told them was an idol. It is tempting simply to shake our heads and consign the whole sad story to the aberrations file, something that inexplicably happened once and surely would never happen again. But if the tragedies of the last century have taught us anything, it is not to be so smug. It will always be necessary to stay on the lookout for Pilgrims attempting to nail their particular flags to the mast. That said, however, Pilgrims are hardly the only extremists out there. When confronted with the question of where our rights come from, there are equally extreme solutions being pushed by the Park Rangers. Let's rejoin the story of Michael Newdow but step back a couple of years in time, to when the Supreme Court chapter in that saga was still but a gleam in Newdow's eye.

CHAPTER THREE

. . . And the Park Rangers Pledge Theirs

Circumstances couldn't have been more different for Michael Newdow and his daughter than they were for the Barnette and Gobitis families. As we've just seen, the first two challenges to the Pledge of Allegiance were desperate lawsuits, filed in dire times. They were brought in World War II–era rural Pennsylvania and West Virginia at a time when grade school Jehovah's Witnesses and their parents across the country were being subjected to astonishingly cruel punishments for refusing to pledge their allegiance to the flag and to the republic for which it stood. In Michael Newdow's 1990s Florida, by contrast, no one had been tarred and feathered. No one's possessions had been burned, and no one had been forced to drink castor oil and marched through town. In fact, no one had been punished at all for not pledging their allegiance to "one nation under God." So unlike in *Barnette* and *Gobitis,* Newdow's challenge to the Pledge began somewhat abstractly. But no one should mistake this rather academic tone for a lack of practical commitment. If the Jehovah's Witness families had been courageous, Newdow and his colleagues were indefatigable. They took their idea of rights every bit as seriously as did the Gobitis and Barnette families. One could, however, be forgiven for wondering just what made Newdow tick.

An Activist's Activist

In 1998 Newdow was a practicing physician who also had a law degree. He was living in Florida and busily preparing a lawsuit. Although it was not yet the Pledge challenge, it too was clearly a long shot. He was going to try, where many before him had failed, to get *In God We Trust* taken off the national currency.

And just what had driven the emergency room doctor to mount an assault on the national motto in the first place? He explains that one day, as he was waiting to buy soap,

> I'm standing in line, I'm looking at the twenty-dollar bill, and it says "In God We Trust." What the heck is this doing here? It just had never hit me. I looked at the ten-dollar bill. "In God We Trust." And the five and the one and all the change. I thought, "What is going on here? I don't trust in God. I'm an American."[1]

So he drew up a lawsuit, patterning it on a case that the Freedom From Religion Foundation (a group that believes in nothing so much as absolute truth-in-labeling) had most recently lost in the Tenth Circuit Court of Appeals in Denver. But then, as he was doing his research, he came across the words *under God* that had been added to the Pledge of Allegiance in 1954 and that were recited daily by public schoolchildren across the country. He shrewdly concluded that the Pledge would make a better target. The national motto, after all, had been on American money for over a century, wasn't recited daily by anybody, and had nothing to do with public schools. So he switched horses and decided to take on the Pledge first.

STANDING AROUND

As it turned out, though, challenging the Pledge was still easier said than done. That was principally because, unlike the Gobitis and Barnette children who had faced real persecution, Newdow had difficulty demonstrating any real injury at all. And without a demonstrable injury, without skin in the game, a party lacks legal standing to bring a lawsuit.

Newdow had three main problems on that score. First, his only daughter was so young she wasn't even enrolled in school yet. Second, she lived in California with her mother, who had legal custody of her, and she rarely saw her father. And third, she wasn't an atheist; her mother was raising her as a Christian and had no objection whatever to her reciting the Pledge. Undaunted, Newdow filed suit in Florida anyway, only to have the trial court promptly dismiss it for lack of standing.

No quitter, Newdow then set about trying to establish his standing. He tried persuading the little girl's mother to enroll her for half of each month in a school in California, where she lived, and the other half of each month in a school in Florida, where he lived. That, of course, went nowhere. So he waited until his daughter was enrolled in a California school, then moved there and filed his lawsuit. As Newdow candidly explained:

> My daughter is in the lawsuit because you need that for standing. I brought this case because I am an atheist and this offends me, and I have

the right to bring up my daughter without God being imposed into her life by her schoolteachers. . . . [S]he did not come and say she was ostracized.[2]

The trial judge took barely more than a page to rule against him.

Still undeterred, Newdow went to the Ninth Circuit Court of Appeals in San Francisco. And there something completely unexpected happened. He won. A three-judge panel split 2–1; struck down the Pledge for its inclusion of the words *under God;* and, invoking the Establishment Clause, prohibited schoolchildren from continuing the recitation that had started school days for roughly half a century.

The ruling caused quite an uproar. The president promptly pronounced it "ridiculous," the U.S. Senate voted 99 to 0 in support of an unedited Pledge, and the House of Representatives expressed its disagreement with the court by a vote of 416 to 3. Nevertheless, after still more legal wrangling, the Ninth Circuit stuck to its guns and refused to rehear the case.

The battle then went to the Supreme Court, which ordered the two sides to argue two questions. Did a parent like Newdow, who lacked legal custody of his child and the authority to determine his child's education or religious upbringing, have standing to challenge the practices of the school that the child's custodial parent had chosen? And, if so, did leading public schoolchildren in the Pledge that included the phrase *under God* violate the Establishment Clause?

Following briefing and argument, the Court reversed the Ninth Circuit's prohibition on including *under God* in the Pledge, but it did so on the narrow (but now familiar) grounds that Newdow lacked sufficient standing to bring the case—this time because he was a noncustodial parent. It never had to reach the more momentous question of whether the Pledge violated the Establishment Clause by including the words *under God*.

A Dogged Pursuit

Still no quitter, Newdow soon teamed up with other atheist parents in California who unquestionably had standing and, acting as their attorney, filed a similar suit yet again in January 2005. This time the Becket Fund (the nonprofit religious liberty law firm which I founded and where I served as president) intervened in the case on behalf of the Knights of Columbus and California public school parents who very much wanted their children to continue pledging their allegiance to a nation whose government acknowledges its proper limits. What was at stake, we explained, was what the next generation is taught about where its rights come from.[3]

Newdow initially prevailed in the federal trial court in California, but we won 2–1 in the Ninth Circuit Court of Appeals in San Francisco, the same court that had previously ruled for Newdow. And we won as well in a parallel case that Newdow had brought in New Hampshire, lost, and then appealed to the First

Circuit in Boston. The Ninth Circuit majority's opinion is particularly enlightening. It holds that Congress had "two main purposes" for having *one nation under God* in the Pledge. The first was "to underscore the political philosophy of the Founding Fathers that God granted certain inalienable rights to the people which the government cannot take away."[4] The second was to "add the note of importance" that "in our culture ceremonial references to God arouse."[5] The First Circuit wasn't quite so expansive in its reasoning but nonetheless solidly upheld the Pledge.

Neither court of appeals, however, has the authority to resolve the question definitively. Only the Supreme Court of the United States can do that.

Newdow initially sought to take both of those losses to the Supreme Court. Then, for some reason, he thought better of it and sought to appeal only the decision from New Hampshire. The Supreme Court declined his invitation to take up that case, which left him legally stymied, for the moment anyway. Nevertheless, he has certainly succeeded in teeing-up the ultimate issue in the culture wars—where do our human and legal rights come from?

Newdow's position, and that of Park Rangers generally, is that rights can be granted only by the state. There are, they insist, no other actors on stage. And the First Amendment, they say, forbids the government from claiming otherwise. The traditional position is that our fundamental human rights—including those *secured* by the First Amendment—are endowed to us by the Creator and that it would be perilous to permit the government ever to repudiate that point. That traditional understanding and the Park Rangers' position cannot both be correct. So which is it? As we're about to see, that is, on several levels, an inescapable question.

CHAPTER FOUR

An Inescapable Question . . .

The seventeenth-century French mathematician and philosopher Blaise Pascal is most famous (some might say infamous) for what has come to be known as Pascal's Wager. Pascal posited that all of us—believers, thinkers, atheists, and agnostics alike—face the same practical choice: Will we live our life *as if* God exists? Or will we conduct ourselves *as if* He does not? Pascal then went on to assert that what a poker player might call the "pot odds" favored piety. That is, the return on a correct bet that God exists would be enormous—eternal happiness—whereas the cost of that bet if it turned out that there was neither God nor afterlife would be much more modest—merely, he said, some quantity of guilty pleasures forgone in the here and now.[1]

You Bet Your Life, So to Speak

That argument remains as controversial today as when it was published in 1669. Many have quipped that, if they were God, the first people they would condemn to Hell would be those who sought to profit from Pascal's Wager. There are others who think more highly of the argument. Nevertheless, regardless of the value of the argument itself, Pascal's underlying insight is sound. No matter how firmly one might hold an intellectual position of agnosticism, not knowing whether there is a God, one cannot live daily life from that perspective. It is simply impossible, in the day-to-day circumstances in which we find ourselves, to prescind from the question of whether there is a Creator who rewards and punishes. We can be truly perplexed over the issue of

God's existence, but in facing the serious choices of daily life—whether to help a stranger in need, whether to cheat or slander someone, and so on—there is no way to abstain or to vote present. We must vote either aye or nay. We all must make moral choices. And, Pascal notes, the possibility of reward or punishment looms large in how we make them. In short, Pascal's position is not that agnostics *ought* to think harder until they conclude whether God exists. It's that, as a practical matter, it's impossible for them or anyone else not to behave in one way or the other, regardless of how refined their reasoning.[2]

What is true of individual human beings is similarly true of governments composed of human beings. Every government necessarily has a position on where its people's rights come from, whether that *de facto* position is articulated or even consciously considered. Every government must either respect its people's rights because they arise from a source higher than and prior to it, or it must admit that it harbors no such principles. In which case, it must concede that all that stands between it and totalitarianism are its own policy choices.

This is not to say, of course, that every state must be a confessional one or else officially atheist. Far from it. In fact, full-fledged confessional or atheist states are, happily, a distinct minority. Confessional states have a very uneven record on the question of conscience rights. England, at least officially, is such a state. And so is Saudi Arabia. They nevertheless hold very different positions on the subject of human rights. On the other hand, officially atheist states' records are not nearly as checkered; they are all but uniformly abysmal. Think Stalin. Or Mao. Or Pol Pot.

The point isn't even that every state must make some sort of formal election for theism generally. Clearly not all states do. Again, the point is simply that every state will necessarily deal with its citizens as if it has made such a choice in one direction or the other. Either it will regard the people as having fundamental—if not always convenient—inalienable human rights, or it will not.

INSECURITY ISSUES

For its part, America has chosen—from the Declaration on—to accept the premise that it is "self-evident" that we are "all . . . created equal" and "endowed by [our] Creator with certain inalienable rights." The Declaration further teaches that the proper role of government is to "secure" the people's rights. Not to "bestow" or "grant" those rights, but to "secure" them. The rights already exist. We need the government only to respect our rights in the way it treats us, and to guard our rights against infringement by others.

The preamble to the Constitution uses the same verb, *secure,* in order to acknowledge that point. Its purpose, it says, is to "secure the Blessings of Liberty." *Blessings* was not an empty word in the eighteenth century. Nor did it equate simply with "good luck." A blessing was a gift from the Creator. It needed only to be *secured* by law.

These points came through loud and clear to the founding generation. In the debate over whether to add a Bill of Rights to the Constitution, Alexander Hamilton argued that it was unnecessary because the preamble already made clear that "the people surrender nothing; and as they retain everything they have no need of particular reservations."[3] Hamilton had long been on record as to just where he thought such rights originated. Before Jefferson had authored the Declaration, Hamilton wrote in a pamphlet defending the justice of a revolution: "The sacred rights of mankind are not to be rummaged for, among old parchments, or musty records. They are written, as with a sunbeam, in the whole volume of human nature, by the hand of the divinity itself; and can never be erased or obscured by mortal power."[4]

When the pro–Bill of Rights forces carried the day, the two final amendments in the Bill of Rights, the Ninth and Tenth Amendments, were added explicitly to deny the notion that the amended Constitution was actually *creating* the rights that it enumerated or that those enumerated rights were all the rights there were. The Ninth Amendment says that "the enumeration in the Constitution, of certain rights, shall not be construed to deny or disparage *others retained* by the people." And the Tenth Amendment provides that "the powers not delegated to the United States by the Constitution, nor prohibited by it to the States, are *reserved* to the States respectively, or to the people." You only "retain" or "reserve" things you already have.

So both the preamble and the Bill of Rights reemphasize what the Declaration had already insisted on: it is not the government, nor even the Constitution, that is the source of our rights. No, the "Blessings of Liberty" come from a higher source. (And lest there be any doubt, as soon as it finished drafting and proposing the Bill of Rights to the states, Congress petitioned President Washington to declare a national day of thanksgiving to God for its successful completion of that task.)

THE PHILOSOPHERS' GOD IN
AMERICAN TRADITION

That idea is not just some quaint intellectual antique. It has been repeated by all three branches of our government and echoes in all fifty state constitutions. It's been repeated by every president, from Washington to Obama. And not just in passing or in obscure speeches to religious groups. The overwhelming majority of presidential inaugural addresses include some reference to God. Each emphasized particular aspects of the relationship between the Creator and creation, whether as the source of rights, of blessing to the country, or of wisdom and guidance.

Take, for instance, John Adams's plea that the "being who is supreme over all, the Patron of Order, the Fountain of Justice, and the Protector in all ages of the world of virtuous liberty, continue his blessing upon this nation."[5] William Henry Harrison took the time in his inaugural to distinguish the "Beneficent Creator" of natural rights found in the Declaration and Constitution from any notion of theocracy: "We admit of no government of divine right, believing that so far as power is concerned the Beneficent Creator has made no distinction amongst men; that all are upon an equality."[6]

John F. Kennedy's inaugural address is one of the most famous. In it he stressed America's continued "belief that the rights of man come not from the generosity of the state, but from the hand of God."[7] Ronald Reagan: "We are a nation under God, and I believe God intended for us to be free."[8] Barack Obama began his second inaugural address by quoting the Declaration, re-emphasizing that freedom is "a gift from God" to be "secured by His people here on Earth."

But by far the most stunning example is Lincoln's second inaugural address. The address, perhaps the greatest oration in American history, turns on Lincoln's assertion that both North and South were being punished by the Almighty for the crime of slavery:

Fondly do we hope—fervently do we pray—
that this mighty scourge of war may speedily
pass away. Yet, if God wills that it continue,
until all the wealth piled by the bondsman's
two hundred and fifty years of unrequited toil
shall be sunk, and until every drop of blood
drawn with the lash, shall be paid by another
drawn with the sword, as was said three thousand years ago, so still it must be said "the
judgments of the Lord, are true and righteous
altogether."[9]

It may be all but incomprehensible to us
today that Lincoln would suggest, in the middle
of the most terrible war in American history, that
the nation deserved the terrors of that war as
punishment for violating the inalienable rights of
the slaves. But that is precisely what he did.

In each of these cases, along with dozens of
other inaugural addresses and other speeches,
our presidents have stood before the country and
renewed the basic premise that we are a country

founded on a system of natural rights that do not derive from the government.

The Supreme Court, for all its vacillations on the religion clauses of the First Amendment, has continued to reaffirm that the Framers did not view mere references to or invocations of God as an "establishment" of religion. Quite the contrary: as even Justice William O. Douglas noted: "the institutions of our society are founded on the belief that there is an authority higher than the authority of the State; . . . that the individual possesses rights, conferred by the Creator, which government must respect."[10] That is, moreover, the very real insight in what is too often assumed to be just a throwaway line by Justice Douglas. Our "institutions" do indeed "presuppose a Supreme Being,"[11] precisely because they presuppose the existence of a source of rights that is prior to the State. As Justice Antonin Scalia notes, the Court has quoted that line with approval several times since.[12]

The Congress has repeatedly harkened back

to the Founder's principle of God given rights. As we'll see in chapter ten, its amendment to, and re-affirmation of, the Pledge of Allegiance is a perfect example.

The same principle is referred to, at least obliquely, in all fifty state constitutions. New York's is a good example ("We The People of the State of New York, grateful to Almighty God for our Freedom, in order to secure its blessings . . .").[13] That God is the source of our rights is an idea deeply rooted in our national identity.

A NATIONAL CREED, SORT OF

B ritish author G. K. Chesterton came to the United States for a national lecture tour in 1921 and was amused to find that he couldn't even get a visa from the American consulate in Britain without answering some pointed questions, including "Are you an anarchist?" Such concern for his "views on the ethical basis of civil authority" surprised him. Chesterton joked with his fellow Europeans that they must not think these questions meant the American Constitution was no better than the Spanish Inquisition. And yet, he wrote,

> The American Constitution does resemble the Spanish Inquisition in this: that it is founded on a creed. America is the only nation in the world that is founded on a creed. That creed is set forth with dogmatic and even theological lucidity in the Declaration of Independence; perhaps the only piece of practical politics that is also theoretical politics and also great literature. It enunciates that all men are equal in their claim to justice, that governments exist to give them that justice, and that their authority is for that reason just.[14]

Chesterton goes on to say that the Declaration, though it mentions God, doesn't provide Americans with any particular religion, but it is significant that Americans have "a creed, if not about divine, at least about human things."

It is wrong, he tells his countrymen, to smugly dismiss the Americans' questions as nonsense: "We do not have any of that nonsense in England because we have never attempted to have any of that philosophy in England."[15]

Where the English nation historically has had Anglicanism, and before that, Catholicism, America instead has a philosophy. And on the basis of that philosophy, our government presumes the existence of a God who endows the people with rights.

Our rights tradition, in other words, presupposes theism. That choice cannot simply be walked back after more than two centuries without abandoning the foundations of the rights themselves. And one of the most terrible lessons of the twentieth century is that a state does not long sustain cognitive dissonance about what rights its people have. Rather, what too often results is the emergence of a regime that resolves the dissonance in its own favor, maximizing its power while diminishing the freedom of the people.

As we'll see in the next chapter, if we ever have to seriously account for our equality or dignity without recourse to the Creator, we are likely, at an absolute minimum, to be greatly embarrassed.

CHAPTER FIVE

. . . With a Great Deal at Stake in the Answer

" There is no God, and Mary is His mother."[1] So Robert Lowell famously quipped about the thought of George Santayana.[2] Woody Allen is said to have taken aim at a similar tension in some parts of the Jewish community: "God might not exist, but we are His chosen people." In a particularly bleak moment, Ely in Cormac McCarthy's *The Road* observes, "There is no God and we are his prophets."[3] A similar cognitive dissonance seems to bedevil Americans who imagine that our traditions of equality and inalienable rights could survive the demise of the Creator who bestows them. So, with a nod to Lowell et al., let's reflect on the consequences of that idea. That is, let's consider the claims that "there is no God and He has created us all equal," and "there is no God and He has endowed us with inalienable rights."

There Is No God, and He Has Created Us All Equal

That "we are all created equal" is one of the things that most identifies us as Americans. As distinct from, say, Saudis, Indians, and even the British, Americans of all ages and circumstances instinctively resist attempts to erect velvet rope lines between classes of people. Discrimination of any sort is seen as one of the worst social offenses one can commit.

In fact, there is such an overwhelming consensus on that point that we would be hardpressed to pinpoint precisely where and when it was that we learned that all of us are equal. It's simply in the air and in the water, we drink it with our mothers' milk. And we profess it proudly, despite the fact that, empirically anyway, its most obvious meaning seems to make little sense. We show up in this life manifestly unequal in all sorts of respects—talent, health, beauty, family influence, financial resources, and so on. Yet we have not abandoned the notion that we're somehow all equal. Quite the contrary, it is a staple of our public discourse. And it remains the argument of choice for those attempting to advance novel legal or social theories. Simply put, America would not be America without the conviction that we're all, in a very important sense, equal.

Plato invented his "myth of the metals" to explain to the common folk why the Guardian class would be privileged and, for the most part, they would not be. The Guardians, according to Plato's myth, were born with gold in their nature. Others had silver, most just bronze. Even in the ancient times, inequality demanded an explanation, something to account for the disparities in human existence.[4]

The same is true, in spades, for twenty-first-century America. Instead of a Platonic apology for inequality, however, we have very nearly its opposite—the idea that the Creator has made us all equal in dignity or, as Lincoln put it, the "proposition" that all are created equal. The king may be better looking than you or more intelligent than you. (Then again, maybe not.) In all events, he is likely to be better dressed than you. But he's not actually one of your "betters," as the British like to say. The Constitution specifies that titles of nobility may never be awarded by the government and foreign titles have no force in America.[5] It's simply "Mr. President" here. And Elton John is really "Sir Elton" only over there.

So we're each equal to the king. And not only that, the waiter, the cook, and the dishwasher are all equal to us. When anyone asks why, the American tradition responds, because God has made us so. Indeed, we don't even feel the need to present argument on the matter. It is, the Declaration assures us, "self-evident." But what if it were to go from self-evident to unthinkable that a Creator has done any such thing? What if the Michael Newdows of this world were to have their way and public recitation of the Pledge of Allegiance or the Declaration of Independence was edited to censor out the offending terms *Creator* in the Declaration and *under God* in the Pledge? What would become of our foundational principle of equality? To say there is no God is to do more than simply tinker with one of the most famous one-liners in history; it is to change the starting point of our whole explanation of who we are as Americans. What answer could ever take its place?

As we saw in the last chapter, America has steadfastly taken the position that there is a Supreme Being who is the source of our rights and the author of our equality. It has repeated that point for well over two hundred years throughout all branches and levels of government. It is the rationale for our ideas of equality and inalienable rights. Practically speaking, there is nothing to replace it. And even if there were, it is probably impossible to walk all this back, slip the foundation out from under our rights theory, and quickly slip in a new one without the entire edifice collapsing in the process.

Amending the Constitution is a straight-forward if difficult process. But how do you go about amending the Constitution's premises? There is no process for that, and surely no consensus for it, either.

THERE IS NO GOD, AND HE HAS ENDOWED US WITH INALIENABLE RIGHTS

Coming up with a different starting point for human rights turns out to be a tall order, in any event. That was precisely the task given to leading thinkers from around the world when they gathered in 1947 under the auspices of the United Nations to determine whether a new consensus on human rights could be achieved.[6] The 1947 UNESCO Committee on the Theoretical Bases of Human Rights, dubbed the Philosophers' Committee, was only partially successful.

Their efforts led to the Universal Declaration of Human Rights, adopted by the UN General Assembly on December 10, 1948. It was lauded around the globe as a watershed moment for international human rights.

Still, their success was limited. They were able to come to a consensus on the *who* and *what* of universal rights but couldn't agree on *how,* in theory, to ground them.[7] French philosopher Jacques Maritain, who was a member of the Philosophers' Committee, summed up the limits this way: "We agree on these rights, on condition that no one asks us why."[8]

To be fair, while the Universal Declaration does not lay out a systematic grounding for human rights, it does hint at one. Still reeling from the horrors of the Holocaust, the General Assembly agreed that, because of the "disregard and contempt for human rights" at the heart of those "barbarous acts which have outraged the conscience of mankind," it was necessary to recognize "the inherent dignity and . . . the equal and inalienable rights of all members of the human family [as] the foundation of freedom, justice, and peace in the world."[9] This notion grounds the basis for justice in the idea of rights, which is straightforward enough. But it remains unclear how rights are connected with "the inherent dignity" of the person.

The Universal Declaration's preamble continues with its intertwining of human rights and human dignity, observing that in the UN Charter "the peoples of the United Nations . . . reaffirmed their faith in fundamental human rights, [and] in the dignity and worth of the human person."[10]

This connection between rights and dignity is no coincidence. As Harvard Law School professor Mary Ann Glendon observes, Maritain himself had insisted that if the future Declaration "were not to be a mere hodgepodge of ideas, it would need a tuning fork or 'key' according to which the rights could be harmonized. Everything depends, [Maritain] said, on 'the ultimate value whereon those rights depend and in terms of which they are integrated by mutual limitations."[11] In other words, if the Declaration could not appeal to an ultimate source of rights, it could, at least, appeal to an "ultimate value" that would make the document internally coherent: "The Universal Declaration belongs to a family of postwar rights instruments that accord their highest priority to human dignity."[12]

So human dignity is the "ultimate value" that gives coherence to human rights. But if rights somehow depend on dignity, where does dignity come from? Once again, the Declaration doesn't specifically say but seems to hint. Article 1 asserts that "[a]ll human beings are born free and equal in dignity and rights. They are endowed with reason and conscience and should act towards one another in a spirit of brotherhood."[13]

To paraphrase Maritain, it seems that, here again, we can achieve consensus that there is such a thing as human dignity (who would admit they oppose it?), just so long as we do not have to answer where that dignity comes from. But if human rights follow from human dignity, then the contours of those rights must depend on the contours of that dignity. Change the basis or scope of human dignity, and the rights can go all wrong.

AT A LOSS

I t's often noted that ideas have consequences. So does the lack of ideas. It is one thing to say that there are no such things as God-given rights or equality, or to go along with the Park Rangers of the world who argue that the Constitution should be "godless" and the country officially agnostic. It is quite another to cope with the consequences that such a tectonic shift would work in how we understand ourselves as individuals and as a nation.

It is no answer to suggest that if we were writing on a blank slate, we could find some way to reground our rights and equality. First, we are not writing on any such blank slate. Far from it. And second, as the UN Philosophers' Committee discovered, it is by no means clear that any such alternative foundation is available. In fact, as Glendon notes,

> It is probable that religion is an important factor in the minimal social cohesion that a heterogeneous society like ours requires. That was the belief of many of this nation's founders, and it is the conclusion reached by a number of the best secular thinkers in Europe, where the trend toward marginalization of religion is more advanced than in the United States. Jürgen Habermas, a professed atheist and political leftist, surprised many of his followers when he announced that he had come to think that the social goods we take for granted in free societies may well have had their source in the legacy of the "Judaic ethic of justice and the Christian ethic of love." In his case, it was concern about biological engineering and the instrumentalization of human life that led him to conclude that the West cannot abandon its religious heritage without endangering

the great social and political advances that are grounded in that heritage. "The liberal state," he has written, "depends in the long run on mentalities that it cannot produce from its own resources."[14]

Agnostic philosopher and former president of the Italian Senate Marcello Pera makes a similar point:

Consider the situation in our liberal states. [T]ypically they are founded on rights that are not legislatively constructed by those same states but have been recognized as natural. For this reason, these rights have been defined as "inalienable," "sacred," "intangible," "nonnegotiable," etc. Thus, the Universal Declaration of Human Rights (1948) speaks of the "*recognition* of the inherent dignity and of the equal and inalienable rights of all members of the human family." The Convention for the Protection of Human Rights and Fundamental Freedoms (1950) speaks of the *"recognition"* of those rights. The European Charter of Fundamental Rights (2000) states that "the Union *recognizes* the rights, freedoms, and principles set out hereafter," and the European Constitution (2004) affirms that "The Union shall *recognize* the rights, freedoms, and principles set out in the Charter of Fundamental Rights." Clearly, the verb "to recognize" means something different from "to concede," "to attribute," or "to emanate." To say that a state "recognizes" (or "safeguards" or "respects") fundamental rights means that those rights belong to its citizens *independently* of the action of that state, and *antecedently* to their condition as citizens. Exactly like the natural law of the liberal tradition.[15]

In short, in Europe as in America, fundamental human rights must be grounded in something or someone prior to the state and higher than the common consensus of the majority. If we have such rights, it is only because we have been "endowed" with them. So Lowell's wit notwithstanding, if there is no God, we have no inalienable rights, and there is no basis for our equality.

And so we run once again headlong into Newdow's Conundrum. Our rights tradition is grounded in theism. But constitutionally, how can that be? After all, as Michael Newdow himself insists, if you can't say "one nation under Jesus," how can you say "one nation under God"?

PART

II

CHAPTER SIX

Thinking About Thinking About God

Religious believers aren't the only ones who talk about God. Thinkers of many faiths and none at all have debated God's existence for centuries, entirely apart from any religious dogmas. Take, for example, an oft-told tale of a Hasidic master and an atheist:

> In the town of Berditchev, the home of the great Hasidic master Reb Levi Yitzhak, there was a self-proclaimed, self-assured atheist, who would take great pleasure in publicly denying the existence of God. One day Reb Levi Yitzhak of Berditchev approached this man

and said, "You know what, I don't believe in the same God that you don't believe in."[1]

They disagreed about whether God existed. But they agreed on who God could never be.

In fact, the idea that it's possible to be rationally convinced that we are the free, intelligent creatures of a free, intelligent Creator, is one with a long and distinguished pedigree.

HIS MOVE

One of the oldest instances of that idea comes from Aristotle. In the fourth century B.C.E., in one of his most difficult works, the *Metaphysics,* he concludes that there is something he calls "God"—remarkably, in the singular, even though in the Athens of his day quite a few different gods, plural, were worshipped in the city's temples. Aristotle's conclusion that there is a God is based solely on reason, unsupported by any religious scripture or divine revelation. To simplify greatly, we can say he argues that the world in which we find ourselves must have had, at its beginning, a "first mover" that set it in motion. "The first mover, then, exists of necessity . . . and it is in this sense a first principle." Aristotle adds that "on such a principle . . . depend the heavens and the world of nature."[2]

That word, *nature,* brings us to the first of two crucial distinctions that underlie the philosophy of God: first, the distinction between nature and convention, and second, the distinction between reason and revelation.

Nature in the thought of Aristotle and the other ancient Greeks meant something different from what we usually mean by that word. While we tend to think of nature as "the great outdoors," a place where plants and animals live undisturbed by humans, the early Greek philosophers had something quite different in mind. It helps to remember that the Greek word for nature gives us our word *physics*. Think Einstein, not Bambi.

Nature in this sense means both the kind of

thing an object is at its very core as well as the end, or final purpose, or *telos,* toward which it is directed. When the Greeks spoke of nature, they were thinking of the whole cosmos, including us, and especially of the order that our reason can discover in the cosmos. Jefferson's "nature and . . . nature's God" in the Declaration of Independence is a perfect example.

The ancient Greek philosophers distinguished this *nature* from *convention. Convention,* then and now, refers to norms that derive not from the object itself but from common agreement among a group of people. The example Aristotle gives is instructive: that a prisoner's ransom be one mina is not indicative of anything called "right by nature." Rather, it is an act of conventional justice. This removes convention, for Aristotle, from transcendent justice and places it squarely within the realm of man-made creation.[3] In Aristotle's day, his fellow citizens of Athens had no shortage of notions about right and wrong and so on. But Aristotle knew that in other cities, other people had quite different notions about these things. What made one a philosopher was one's willingness to suspend assent to such conventional ideas and to think through the issues independently in order to determine the nature of them.

Why bother? In order to discover even more important truths. As Leo Strauss puts it, the "discovery of nature" brings with it the possibility of discovering truths that are "trans-historical, trans-social, trans-moral, and trans-religious."[4] In other words, to get to the bottom of things. (Today, as in ancient Athens, thinkers aren't always thanked for those efforts. Aristotle himself at one point had to grab his family and flee the city for fear that he would meet the same fate as Socrates, who was put to death by the Athenians on charges of not believing in the city's gods and of corrupting the youth.)

Among the big questions Aristotle insisted on thinking through for himself was the question "Where did everything come from?" The essence of his conclusion—that our experience of the world leads us to conclude that it does not exist as it is accidentally—is still enjoying a good run in a variety of different forms. It has been debated, criticized, revised, and reformulated ever since.

Prove It

Thomas Aquinas restated Aristotle's argument in his famous "five proofs" of the existence of God.[5] The five proofs—"From Motion" (anything in motion needs something to start it moving; there must be a "First Mover" to start it all); "From Efficient Cause" (similar to "From Motion"—every effect must be caused by something); "From Possibility and Necessity"; "From Perfection"; and "From Design"—in turn, have themselves been criticized, tweaked, and restated for the past 750 years. For example, current versions of the fifth, "From Design," argument proceed from the premise that the world's beauty points to the existence of an original artist. (And there is intriguing evidence that in abstract mathematics choosing the more beautiful potential solution to a problem leads to the correct answer in a statistically significant percentage of cases.)

That these "proofs" are eight centuries old does not necessarily mean they've lost their vitality. In fact, some say advancement of our scientific understanding can make the cases for these proofs even stronger. The obituary of the famous philosopher Antony Flew tells the story in terms of his life. Flew spent most of his career arguing against the existence of God, only to do a dramatic about-face near the end of his life. He credited his shift primarily to Aquinas's arguments from motion and design, concluding that his own research into DNA had "shown, by the almost unbelievable complexity of the arrangements which are needed to produce life, that intelligence must have been involved." In addition, he became convinced that current science could not on its own explain the beginnings of life: "I have been persuaded that it is simply out of the question that the first living matter evolved out of dead matter and then developed into an extraordinarily complicated creature."[6]

In between Aristotle and Aquinas, another great thinker, Anselm of Canterbury, offered a different philosophical argument for the existence of God, one known as the "ontological argument."[7] Simply put (again, no doubt too simply), Anselm begins with an understanding of God as that "than which nothing greater can be conceived." Roughly speaking, God is the best thing you can imagine. At this point, God only exists in your mind. But you can imagine a God even better than that, a God who isn't just a figment of your imagination, but actually exists in reality. And so, Anselm concluded, God must exist because otherwise he wouldn't be the best thing you can imagine.

Now that strikes some as more akin to a knock-knock joke than to a viable argument. Aquinas, for one, was far from convinced. On the other hand, plenty of other intellectual heavyweights, including René Descartes, have thought Anselm was on to something and produced their own versions of the ontological argument.

When Aquinas and Anselm offered their

"proofs," they were seeking to discover the truth using reason alone, which is something distinct from contemplating revelation as a theologian. The difference was already clear in Aristotle's *Metaphysics,* where he distinguishes the first philosophers, who "discoursed on nature," from others who preceded them and "discoursed on gods."[8]

BELIEVERS AND THINKERS

Another common name for this distinction between philosophy and theology is "reason versus revelation." Philosophy operates on the basis of reason. It entails using our rational powers to make sense of things that we can clearly see before us. Theology, by contrast, begins not with our observations but with our beliefs, with things that we hold to be just as true as, say, the multiplication tables, but that we believe have been revealed to us by a supernatural source; for example, the Christian revelation that

Jesus of Nazareth is the Son of God and the Second Person of the Blessed Trinity.

Technically, according to the philosophical tradition, one can't "know" and "believe" the same thing in the same way at the same time. A simple example: If someone tells you that 4,386 multiplied by 9,782 equals 42,903,852, at first you may believe him or her. But later, if you work it out yourself and see that it's true, you no longer *believe* the other person's answer; you *know* it yourself. Knowledge and belief aren't always at odds, but they are different.

And when you think about it, each of us believes things every day. We plug an address into a GPS and believe that the little map that pops up will eventually get us there. High school chemistry students accept on faith the results of experiments recounted by their teachers. In these cases, we are choosing to believe something someone else tells us. Belief in this sense makes up a rather large part of the information we assume to be true on a day-to-day basis. Unless you're a structural engineer, you don't *know* that the bridge is going to hold up the weight of your car, but you do *believe* that the engineer who designed it does.

Rational knowledge, by contrast, involves knowing something is true because it's been proven to you. If you follow the GPS, and it eventually ("recalculating") gets you where you intended to go, you no longer *believe* the GPS route is accurate; you *know* it. If the chemistry students repeat their teacher's experiment and get the same results, the chemistry students no longer *believe* the results to be true because of their faith in their teacher; now they *know* the results are true.

Some thinker-believers like Maimonides, a Jew, and Thomas Aquinas, a Christian, were skilled in both philosophy and theology, but they also were careful to distinguish them. Aquinas points out to his fellow believers that the claims of Christian revelation can be divided into two sets. The first set are the claims of Christianity that even nonbelieving thinkers like Aristotle could reason to without the aid of revelation; for example, God exists and is good. The second, and larger, set of Christian claims are things that reason alone could never smoke out—things like the Trinity or the Incarnation. Aquinas calls these "Mysteries of Faith." They're conclusions that can't be arrived at except by faith in Divine Revelation.

Admittedly, there have been times when philosophers have twisted themselves into knots that look ridiculous, leading some believers to reject philosophy as worthless. At the beginning of the Protestant Reformation, Martin Luther recoiled from the abstruse Scholastic philosophy of his day. He urged believers to study Scripture and pass on Aristotle. In the nineteenth century, the existentialist Søren Kierkegaard would likewise turn against the then-dominant philosophy of German Idealism and urge a "leap" of faith.

Intellectual historian Étienne Gilson points out that this tendency can be found among some Christians throughout history. At least as far back as the second century C.E., Tertullian warned his fellow believers about the "dangers" of thinkers like Aristotle, who had invented "dialectics, the art of building up and pulling down, an art so far-fetched in its conjectures, so harsh in its arguments, so productive of contentions— embarrassing even to itself, retracting everything, and really treating of nothing!"[9]

Critics of philosophy can also cite certain passages in the New Testament as evidence. The Apostle Paul warned the Colossians, "See to it that no one makes a prey of you by philosophy and empty deceit, according to human tradition, according to the elemental spirits of the universe, and not according to Christ" (Colossians 2:8). Elsewhere Paul added that "the foolishness of God is wiser than men" (1 Corinthians 1:25).

And yet, for all the risk that philosophizing may lead some people astray, there is no shortage of serious believers who see a role for philosophy. The Apostle Paul himself, although he warned about the danger that philosophy might obscure faith, nonetheless argued that we can discern God in the world. That's why Paul condemns those who "suppress the truth. For what can be known about God is plain to them, because God has shown it to them. Ever since the creation of the world his invisible nature, namely, his eternal power and deity, has been clearly perceived in the things that have been made" (Romans 1:18–20).

As we'll see, this distinction between philosophy and theology, between what can rationally be concluded and what must be taken on faith, is an important one. It means that you and I can disagree profoundly about theology, and yet agree about a very important point of political philosophy. That is, every person should enjoy the natural rights to life, liberty, and the pursuit of happiness because it is self-evident that they are gifts that were "endowed" to each of us by our "Creator."

The philosophical debates on the existence of God haven't stopped since the Founders' time. Albert Einstein grappled with the issue in the last century and declared himself on the side of the rationalists who think that there is *only* the God of nature. That is, he was convinced of the existence of a "God who reveals Himself in the orderly harmony of what exists, not in a God who concerns Himself with fates and actions of human beings."[10]

The mathematician Kurt Gödel, another of the twentieth century's greatest minds and a colleague of Einstein at Princeton, held similar views, but closer to those of conventional religious believers: "I am convinced of the afterlife, independent of theology. If the world is rationally constructed, there must be an afterlife."[11]

WHAT WE DIDN'T INVENT AND OUGHT TO OBEY

Perhaps the most accessible thinker on this subject (maybe because he was one of the few *trying* to be accessible) was C. S. Lewis. Lewis begins his famous book *Mere Christianity* by reasoning about a phenomenon we all observe in ourselves: our innate sense of right and wrong. He notes that we often choose to do things that we're convinced are wrong, even things we may have publicly denounced as wrong. Yet even when we evade and rationalize, he points out, we bear witness through that very rationalization to "a real law which we did not invent and which we know we ought to obey."[12]

What, Lewis asks, does this tell us "about the universe we live in"? Lewis proceeds, still without appealing to any revelation, to make logical inferences from what he has observed about this built-in moral law. At this point, he is only far enough along in his story to be a Something-ist himself. "I am not yet within a hundred miles of the God of Christian theology," he confesses. "All I have got to is a Something which is . . . urging me to do right and making me feel responsible and uncomfortable when I do wrong."

He continues his reasoning: "I think we have to assume it is more like a mind than it is like anything else we know—because after all the only other thing we know is matter and you can hardly imagine a bit of matter giving instructions."[13]

Lewis is clear about the limits of this kind of reasoning. It won't substitute for revelation; it's not something you can build your life around:

We have not yet got as far as the God of any actual religion, still less the God of that particular religion called Christianity. We have only got as far as a Somebody or Something behind the Moral Law. We are not taking anything from the Bible or the Churches, we are trying to see what we can find out about this Somebody on our own steam.[14]

Lewis then explains that, based on this limited knowledge, no one should take comfort in what has been discovered so far in his argument, because our unaided reasoning doesn't let us "see" clearly enough to know if the Something behind the moral law is a person, much less if it is a person who is willing to forgive us for our repeated violations of it. To find an answer to those questions, Lewis concludes, you need to encounter his "real subject," namely, Christianity. So why did he bother with all that philosophy to start with? "My reason," Lewis tells us, "was that Christianity simply does not make sense until you have faced the sort of facts I have been describing."[15]

He was not writing on a blank slate. As we've seen, thinkers within the Judeo-Christian tradition, as well as thinkers outside of it, had long held that there are some aspects of God that can in principle be known by human reason alone. From the Apostle Paul to Thomas Aquinas and Moses Maimonides, a great many thinkers down through the ages have agreed. Among the attributes of God that can be known by reason alone, according to their view, are that God exists, He is One, He is good, and He is just. He is, in Pascal's words, the God of the philosophers—or as we say here, the Philosophers' God.

Nonetheless, the tradition holds that there are many things about God that cannot be known by our reason alone but can be assented to only by faith in revelation. For Christians, these include "the Trinity, the Incarnation, the redemptive death of Christ on the Cross, his Resurrection and Ascension into glory, the institution of the Church, the sacraments, the bestowal of grace, and the beatific vision."[16] Within the Jewish tradition, Maimonides emphasized how little we can affirmatively say about God, and how we should instead stick to negative descriptions (He is not finite, not bound by time, not ignorant, etc.). In short, it is the conviction of a large contingent of thinkers, both religious believers and otherwise, that human reason alone can uncover the fact that God exists but cannot by itself penetrate the mystery of who God is.

They can say only that He is the Philosophers' God.

A FAINT SKETCH

To be clear, the Philosophers' God is not a different God than the Living God whom believers embrace. He is, rather, only as much of the Living God as can be known through reason alone. The portrait of God that these philosophers are able to draw, when left completely to their own devices, is not much to look at. In fact, it's not really a portrait at all. It's more like a rough sketch of a poorly lit profile, glimpsed at a distance. Indeed, this sketch is so faint that the philosophers rarely even attempt to name its subject. Instead He is traditionally called merely the "God of the philosophers" in Pascal's famous phrase, or the "unmoved mover" in Aristotle's writing, or "Nature's God" in the Founders' terms. That's about as far as their purely rational proofs can take them.

Now if the philosophers can't prove that the Nature's God they've sketched *is,* say, the God of Abraham, Isaac, and Jacob, they just as surely can't prove that He's *not.* So there is nothing whatever to stop believers of various stripes from completing the sketch in their own minds, from their own faith, perhaps smiling to themselves that they would recognize that profile anywhere.

In short, all believers in God are theists, but not all theists must be believers. They can simply be thinkers, if that's as far as their lights lead. It's a question of respecting the distinction between *believing* in God and *being convinced,* or knowing, of God's existence. Believing is a function of faith. Knowing is a function of proof—of rational conclusion. One can be *both* a believer in God and be rationally convinced of His existence—plenty of people are. The point is that one doesn't *have* to be a believer to be convinced. Without adhering to any religious tradition, one can be *rationally convinced—and reasonably assert*—that there is a Supreme Being, a Cosmic Something, a Philosophers' God. And therefore, one can be rationally convinced that there's a transcendent source of our equality and rights. That point turns out to be a very important one. Why? Because, as we'll see, it means that the existence of the God who is the source of our rights—the Creator in the Declaration of Independence tradition—need be advanced only as an intellectual proposition rather than as a religious dogma. And that makes the Philosophers' God a potential solution to some of the thorniest questions we face.

But we're getting ahead of ourselves.

CHAPTER SEVEN

The Education of the Founders

The Founders were heirs of the intellectual tradition of "thinking about thinking about God" that we encountered in the last chapter. With the rapid spread of the college system across the colonies, and the high regard for learning generally, most of those who gathered to debate and sign the Declaration of Independence and to draft the Constitution had enjoyed a robust education. While eighteenth-century American colleges were primarily preparing men for the ministry, they were also providing a broad liberal arts education to gentlemen who would be leaders in society.[1]

THE FOUNDERS GO TO COLLEGE

The establishment of Harvard College in 1636 marked the beginning of formal higher education in the colonies.[2] Joining soon after were William and Mary, Yale, the College of New Jersey (Princeton), the University of Pennsylvania, the College of Rhode Island (Brown), and King's College (Columbia).[3] Those colleges and others sought to develop educated gentlemen by uniting the old Scholastic tradition from medieval Europe with the emerging "New Learning."[4] Originally, colleges were structured around a tutorial model, where a tutor would guide a student through the entirety of his education. The later introduction of the professorial model allowed the teachers to focus their efforts ever deeper in a particular subject, allowing students to circulate among them.[5]

Most students continuing on to college were in their midteens, some as young as fourteen.[6] They were required to learn Latin and usually Greek as well. Studying the classical languages was required as much for mastering the ancient writings as it was for learning to translate.[7] (Some colleges even fined students for using anything but Latin in their studies and interactions.)[8] The curriculum from the seventeenth century into the eighteenth century was based on the *Quadrivium*—arithmetic, geometry, music, and astronomy—the subjects collectively known as the "place where four roads meet" that formed the base of a classical education, and the *Trivium*, which included rhetoric as well as grammar and logic.[9] Many of the readings were classical texts and literature on virtue, ethics, and politics. The Founders read such authors as Thucydides, Plutarch, and Cicero as well as the history of the ancient world by Herodotus.[10]

The educational track at eighteenth-century Harvard looked something like this: The first year began with Latin readings including Virgil, Homer, and Cicero. It also included study of the Greek New Testament, Hebrew, and logic. In the second year they would continue with the studies of the previous year but add physics. By the third year they were studying not just physics but ethics and metaphysical ideas. The fourth year included a review of basic concepts, studies of the past years, and additions of studies in geometry and astronomy. Throughout their education, they also spent time studying divinity as well as disputation.[11]

The curriculum was geared toward a rising interest in the sciences. The college education of the Founders culminated in the period in which the old Scholastic thought met with emerging science. The combination of the liberal arts curriculum of the past tradition and the new enlightened studies ably prepared one for any number of professional careers—as evidenced by many of the Founders continuing studies in law and medicine.[12]

PROVE GOD'S EXISTENCE
(USE BOTH SIDES IF NECESSARY)

As we've seen, one needn't believe in a particular faith in order to reasonably consider of the idea of a Supreme Being. It does not require belief that everything in existence was fashioned in exactly 144 hours and is just over six thousand years old. Nor does it require belief that Moses parted the Red Sea or that Krishna was born from the mind of Vasudeva into the womb of Devaki. One need not believe any faith tradition's account of how we came to be, much less the process by which everything else came to be as well, to be convinced that we were in fact not accidental. In fact, one need not *believe* anything at all to be *convinced*. This distinction—between believing and knowing—is at the heart of the matter.

Even though they didn't adhere to the same theology, people like Thomas Jefferson, James Madison, and George Washington recognized their common intellectual inheritance of the Philosophers' God—an idea by then already steeped in centuries of intense discussion among some of the most esteemed minds in history. (The related idea—that human beings therefore have rights whose source lies in a power higher than the State—has similarly ancient roots, as we'll see in the next chapter.)

The Founders' studies melded a classical education with the thought of the Enlightenment to forge a broad liberal arts education. And it was one that no one thought to question the relevance of. It immediately impacted their political ideas, their careers, and their lives as gentlemen, in the growing American colonies, where all sorts of new things were seeming to be increasingly possible. America was a new experiment in old ideas.

Natural Philosophy

As we've seen, Aristotle's conviction that there must be an Unmoved Mover was entirely a rational conclusion, not a religious belief. Neither of the treatises in which he discusses it is called *I Believe in the Unmoved Mover*. They're called *Physics* and *Metaphysics*, respectively. Aristotle doesn't cite any of the ancient myths in support of his conclusion. Nor does he claim any revelation. He simply reasons his way through a philosophical argument based on logic and observation. So did Anselm and Aquinas. And, in its own way, so did the Enlightenment. René Descartes, one of history's greatest mathematicians and the thinker who's often called the "father of modern philosophy," led the Enlightenment in developing a "natural philosophy" that attempted to unite new scientific knowledge about the universe—arriving by the boatload in those days—with philosophical inquiry. He also provided a reworked version of Anselm's ontological argument for God's existence.[13] He began with his clear idea of God as a "supremely perfect being" distinct from himself. Now, that idea did not originate with him. So God has to exist, he concluded.

Shortly afterward, another rationalist philosopher, Gottfried Leibniz, who was yet another giant in the history of mathematics, penned the classic question "Why is there something rather than nothing?" He responded to it by critiquing Descartes's ontological proof and offering his own version instead.[14]

The careful study of natural philosophy heavily influenced the thoughts and beliefs of America's founding generation. While most associated with physics, natural philosophy emphasized the relationship of philosophy and science generally.[15] It was a study that sought to understand and formulate ideas about the natural world's existence and causation within it. But, as we'll see, it also provided a springboard for the Framers' political ideas.

Though there were intellectual strains of natural philosophy percolating in the French Enlightenment, it was the British philosophers who grappled with the subject the most. Philosopher Helmut Moritz notes the "proud English tradition" of the term *natural philosophy:* "physicists from Isaac Newton to W. Thomson (Lord Kelvin) used it for what we would today call 'theoretical physics with a philosophical touch.'"[16]

And unlike its French counterpart, the British enlightenment—and its expansion into the colonies—maintained a more nuanced understanding of the relationship between nature and nature's God, between rational order and a rational Order-er. Historian and philosopher Sara Gronim summarizes: "natural philosophy was always believed to be a route to the deeper understanding of God's nature. Far from emptying the natural world of its spiritual significance, natural philosophers affirmed the natural world as a text of God."[17]

Of all the natural philosophers, perhaps none

was more significant for shaping the natural philosophy views of the Founders than Sir Isaac Newton.[18] What differentiated Newton from the other natural philosophers of his time, and what made him a favorite of the Founders, was that his writings combined philosophical theory with mathematical principles and physical observation to make for a comprehensive, practical, unified way of making sense of the natural world. Indeed, Newton's *Principia* was one of the guiding lights of colonial college curricula and would become one of the most influential books, as evidenced by the Founders' studies and thoughts.[19]

And though his work has been championed by Park Rangers as an example of science and reason replacing any talk of God,[20] Newton understood his research within the context of uncovering the rational order of a rational creator: "This most beautiful system of the sun, planets, and comets, could only proceed from the counsel and dominion of an intelligent and powerful Being."[21]

Jefferson named *Principia* as one of his favorite books (among his collection of nearly 6,500). He had a portrait of Newton hanging in his home.[22] Many think Jefferson probably had Newton in mind when he referred, in the preamble to the Declaration of Independence, to "Laws of Nature." Putting that in the plural, *laws,* not the singular *law,* suggests that Jefferson was thinking not just of the common law but of Newton's various physical laws as well.[23]

Adams was also a great admirer of Newton and natural philosophy. At Harvard, he noted: "next to the ordinary routine of classical studies, mathematics and natural philosophy were my favorite pursuits."[24] He kept a diary of lectures on Newtonian laws of motion and how they supported his ideas about a system of balance in government. Later on during the Constitutional Convention, Adams recalled how Franklin had "recollected one of Sir Isaac Newton's laws of motion, namely, 'that reaction must always be equal and contrary to action,' or there can never be any rest."[25]

Natural philosophy made its debut in the

American academy at William and Mary in 1711 with Professor Tanaquil Le Fevre.[26] Harvard began its Hollis Professorship of Mathematics and Natural Philosophy under Isaac Greenwood in 1727, and later John Winthrop in 1738,[27] who would become friends with Washington, Franklin, and Adams.[28] The most influential professor for the Founders was William Small, who became professor of natural philosophy at William and Mary in 1758 and befriended Jefferson. In his autobiography, Jefferson credited Small with his "first views of the expansion of science and of the system of things in which we are placed." Jefferson said his friendship with Small "probably fixed the destiny of my life."[29]

Many of the Founders attended one of these colleges in America. Attending college at all was still a relatively rare feat; at the time of the Revolution there were only about twenty-five hundred college graduates on this side of the Atlantic.[30] So the fact that twenty-seven of the fifty-six signers of the Declaration of Independence graduated from college either in America or Europe[31] is a sign of their collective intellectual firepower.

To be sure, the other twenty-nine signers were no intellectual slouches. They were the products of a primary education that left them well versed in the liberal arts and natural philosophy.[32] It's a near certainty that everyone there at the Constitutional Convention would at some point in their lives have read the works of Homer and Cicero, Aristotle and Aquinas, Descartes and Spinoza.[33]

All of this is to say that by the latter half of the eighteenth century, natural philosophy was firmly rooted in the minds of nearly all the central characters surrounding the American founding (and most of those on the fringes as well). Harvard had a president, four tutors, and six professors engaged in the study of natural philosophy.[34] By the time Jefferson wrote in the Declaration of Independence that "all men are created equal," six of the eight colonial colleges had professorships of mathematics and natural philosophy.[35]

From ancient Aristotle and medieval Aquinas to enlightened Descartes and naturalist Newton, the intellectual proposition of the existence of a Supreme Being had enjoyed a run of respectability for the two thousand years or so leading up to the founding. As the various players gathered to sign the Declaration of Independence and later to hold the Constitutional Convention, many of them had already spent a good deal of time thinking through the logical conclusions of such a claim. These conclusions framed the way in which they would forge a nation founded on natural rights endowed to all—a nation, in other words, "under God."

CHAPTER EIGHT

---

*Framing a Nation Under God: The
Political Philosophy of the Founders*

G reat statesmen (and plenty not so great)
have long grappled with the fundamental
questions of society: Why does government exist,
and what place or meaning does it have in our
lives? What are the origins of government and
laws? Then, what is the appropriate nature and
aim of government? How can government really
serve, as well as recognize, human nature?

By the time of the American founding, thinkers had been posing these questions, in theory at
least, for the better part of two millennia. The
ancients, the medievals, and the Enlightened had
all grappled with them. Their theories had often

been ignored in practice—until the Founders set about actively building a state according to them. It was their statecraft, not their philosophy, that was the most revolutionary.

SOMETHING OLD, SOMETHING NEW . . .

Consider this passage from Seneca, a stoic philosopher in Rome who lived from around 3 B.C.E. to 65 C.E.: "This was the intention of the great creator of the universe . . . that only the most worthless of our possessions should fall under the control of another. All that is best for a man lies beyond the power of other men, who can neither give it nor take it away."[1] Now listen to that idea echo in James Madison's observation that every man has "a property in his rights." Those rights, Madison admitted, may not be respected "where an excess of power prevails," but the end of government—what it is always and everywhere *supposed* to do—is "to protect property of every sort," including the "rights of individuals." And so "that alone is a *just* government, which *impartially* secures to every man, whatever is his *own*."[2]

For Madison, as for Seneca seventeen centuries earlier, our greatest possessions are the rights *endowed* to us by our Creator. They may be insecure, they may even be violated ruthlessly by force, but another person cannot truly take them away, because their origin lies in something higher than the person who possesses them or the person who violates them.

This understanding is also found in Cicero, the great Roman statesman and political philosopher who died in 43 B.C.E. He was one of the greatest champions of republican government in the ancient world and is frequently cited by America's Founders. Here is his famous distillation of the natural law:

> True law is right reason conformable to nature, universal, unchangeable, eternal, whose commands urge us to duty, and whose prohibitions restrain us from evil. Whether it enjoins or

forbids, the good respect its injunctions, and the wicked treat them with indifference. This law cannot be contradicted by any other law, and is not liable either to derogation or abrogation. Neither the senate nor the people can give us any dispensation for not obeying this universal law of justice. It needs no other expositor and interpreter than our own conscience. It is not one thing at Rome, and another at Athens; one thing to-day, and another to-morrow; but in all times and nations this universal law must forever reign, eternal and imperishable. It is the sovereign master and emperor of all beings. God himself is its author, its promulgator, its enforcer. And he who does not obey it flies from himself, and does violence to the very nature of man.[3]

No wonder Thomas Jefferson insisted that his Declaration harmonized with Cicero. The Roman statesman could not be more clear: Right and wrong in their essentials do not change, not across time or across geographical boundaries.

What is just and true by nature, he said, comes to us from God and remains true whether or not we obey it.

In respecting our rights and duties, according to Cicero, we are both being true to ourselves and being true to our Creator. We are, in short, obeying the law under God.

UNDER GOD: THE BACKSTORY

This brings us to the way in which the phrase *under God* came to stand as shorthand for natural rights/natural law political philosophy. It's a surprisingly storied legal and political tradition that begins nearly four hundred years before the first Pilgrims arrived at Plymouth.[4]

The first recorded use of the phrase *under God* in Anglo-American legal history comes in the earliest known compendium of English law, Henry of Bracton's *De Legibus et Consuetudinibus Angliæ* (On the Laws and Customs of England), written in the 1230s. Bracton states unequivocally, "The king must not be under man but under God and under the law, because law makes the king."[5] Since the king embodied the government in his person at that time, this first English legal writer was already limiting government by declaring it to be "under God and under the law." When these words were written roughly eight centuries ago, they caused little outrage or astonishment, because even in the 1200s the idea they expressed was a very old and familiar one—at least in theory.

In 1607 Sir Edward Coke, an English lawyer considered to be the greatest jurist of the Elizabethan and Jacobean eras, cited Bracton's phrase and made sure that the point wasn't only theoretical. He used his power as Chief Justice of the Court of Common Pleas to overrule the king's findings and unilaterally limit the king's power to rule. Coke's claim didn't exactly please King James I, who warned Coke he was in danger of committing treason, a crime that merited an especially unpleasant punishment in the seventeenth century. As Coke recalled the incident:

the King was greatly offended [at my claim to overrule his findings], and said, that then he should be under the Law, which was Treason to affirm, as he said; To which I said, that Bracton saith, *Quod Rex non debetesse sub homine, sed sub Deo et Lege.* [The King ought not be under man, but under God and the Law.][6]

The fact that Coke lived to tell this tale shows that even a touchy monarch, irritated by a challenge that confronted him nearly two centuries before the Declaration of Independence, still recognized he had to acknowledge a power higher than himself.

The next great English jurist after Coke was William Blackstone, whose *Commentaries on the Laws of England*, first published in 1765, exercised enormous influence on America's Founders. Indeed, the Supreme Court still refers to Blackstone as "the preeminent authority on English law for the founding generation."[7] Blackstone championed the same principles of limited government that Bracton and Coke had insisted upon.[8] The "law of nature," Blackstone declared, had its source in a "supreme being" and is "impressed" into every human being.[9] For that reason, all laws derived their authority not from human power but from the higher "law of nature":

> This law of nature, being co-eval with mankind and dictated by God himself, is of course superior in obligation to any other. It is binding over all the globe in all countries, and at all times; no human laws are of any validity, if contrary to this: and such of them as are valid derive all their force, and all their authority, mediately or immediately, from this original.[10]

Blackstone's formulation thus puts human laws "under God," denying their validity if they run contrary to the law of nature.

Note that Blackstone is not invoking, say, the Church of England's theology to justify this natural law principle. No, it is "nature" as human reason encounters it and understands it that grounds this principle. Note also that for Blackstone, a law contrary to the natural law is invalid even if that law were passed by Blackstone's own British Parliament against the rights of the Crown's colonists in America.

Blackstone's understanding of the nature and limits of governmental power suffused the intellectual world of the Founders. The Declaration of Independence is perhaps the paradigmatic restatement of this philosophy. Jefferson's defense of the American rebellion proceeds from the "self-evident" truth that all persons "are endowed by their Creator with certain unalienable Rights." Proceeding from this premise, the Declaration explains that these God-given rights provided a basis for Americans to reject a tyrannical government and assume the "equal station to which the Laws of Nature and of Nature's God entitle them."

Of course, Jefferson and the other Founders were not working from scratch. Jefferson later said that the Declaration aimed to capture "the

harmonizing sentiments of the day, whether expressed in conversation, in letters, printed essays,
or in the elementary books of public right, as
Aristotle, Cicero, Locke, Sidney, etc."[11]

We already have a sense of what Jefferson
meant in referring to Aristotle and Cicero. As for
John Locke, we see in the Declaration an allu-
sion to his understanding of the right of a people
to rebel against the government if it violates the
law of nature: "I will not dispute now, whether
princes are exempt from the laws of their country; but this I am sure, they owe subjection to the
laws of God and nature. Nobody, no power, can
exempt them from the obligations of that eternal
law."[12] What's more, "Whence it is plain, that
shaking off a power, which force, and not right,
hath set over any one, though it hath the name of
rebellion, yet is no offence before God, but is that
which he allows and countenances, though even
promises and covenants, when obtained by force
have intervened."[13]

Jefferson similarly relied on the thoughts of
English political thinker Algernon Sidney, who

had been executed in 1683 for allegedly plotting to overthrow the English government. Part of the evidence introduced against him in court was his statement that "the liberties of nations are from God and nature, not from kings,"[14] a statement that, in more peaceful times, might have occasioned less opposition. We can hear Sidney's influence on Jefferson: "Can the liberties of a nation," Jefferson would ask, "be thought secure when we have removed their only firm basis, a conviction in the minds of the people that these liberties are of the gift of God?"[15]

A REVOLUTION UNDER GOD

Considering how central the ideas of God-given rights and natural law were to the Founders, it is not surprising that the phrase *under God* turns up frequently in the writings of the revolutionaries. So, for example, on July 2, 1776, the day when the Continental Congress voted for independence but two days before the

Declaration was adopted, George Washington used the phrase in his general orders to the soldiers risking their lives for that independence:

> The fate of unborn Millions will now depend, *under God,* on the Courage and Conduct of this army—Our cruel and unrelenting Enemy leaves us no choice but a brave resistance, or the most abject submission; this is all we can expect—We have therefore to resolve to conquer or die.[16]

A week later Washington again used the phrase *under God* in his general orders of July 9, 1776, when he ordered the Declaration of Independence to be read to all the troops: "The General hopes this important Event will serve as a fresh incentive to every officer, and soldier, to act with Fidelity and Courage, as knowing that now the peace and safety of his Country depends (under God) solely on the success of our arms."[17]

At war's end, the Continental Congress commissioned James Madison, Alexander Hamilton, and future Chief Justice Oliver Ellsworth to draft an "Address to the States, by the United States in Congress Assembled." The address, written in Madison's hand, ended with a resounding affirmation of the idea that rights inhere in human nature and proceed from their "Author":

> Let it be remembered finally, that it has ever been the pride and boast of America, that the rights for which she contended were the rights of human nature.
>
> By the blessings of the Author of these rights on the means exerted for their defence, they have prevailed against all opposition, and form the basis of thirteen independent states.[18]

Madison reinforced his sentiment in a document written under his own name and delivered to the General Assembly of Virginia:

> It is unalienable also, because what is here a right towards men, is a duty towards the Creator. It is the duty of every man to render to

the Creator such homage and such only as he believes to be acceptable to him. This duty is precedent, both in order of time and in degree of obligation, to the claims of Civil Society. Before any man can be considered as a member of Civil Society, he must be considered as a subject of the Governour of the Universe.[19]

Madison and Hamilton thus agreed with Jefferson that the American Revolution was a fight for "the rights of human nature" and that those rights had an "Author" higher than King George III, Parliament, or any other purely human institution.

What's more, the conclusion that those rights had such an author was not a religious idea but a philosophical one. Perhaps the most striking example is a particular juxtaposition between God and religion in Jefferson's Virginia Bill for Establishing Religious Freedom. The bill's argument begins with the premise "Whereas Almighty God hath created the mind free," and goes on to argue shortly thereafter that "our civil rights have no dependence on our religious opinions, any more than our opinions in physics or geometry."[20] Jefferson clearly thought that the notion that God had created the mind free was not a "religious opinion." It was the same sort of "self-evident" principle that he used to anchor his argument in the Declaration.

In sum, there can be little doubt that at the time the Constitution was drafted, the idea of God-given natural rights was the fundamental premise of America's political philosophy.

CHAPTER NINE

You Say Deist, I Say Theist

Wait a minute. Isn't all this talk about philosophy, natural theology, faith, and reason just a set of euphemisms for good old-fashioned Deism? Deists held, didn't they, that there's no such thing as revelation, only evidence of a grand watchmaker who had wound up the world, set it running, and then moved on? Benjamin Franklin was an acknowledged Deist, wasn't he? Wasn't Jefferson one, too? So isn't the Philosophers' God really just the Deists' deity, and for that matter, doesn't that make the Declaration of Independence just a Deist document? And if not, what's the difference?

{ 131 }

True, Franklin was a Deist (after his fashion), and Jefferson was a quasi-Deist, at least some of the time. Stephen Hopkins of Rhode Island was a Deist, and John Adams is generally thought to have been influenced by Deism. But the ideas they shared in common with the other Founders that are written into the Declaration, and have been repeated ever since, didn't originate in Deism but in theism. And the Philosophers' God isn't limited by Deism's doctrines.

The Deism that was attractive to Franklin and friends was a relatively short-lived religious movement that had originated in seventeenth-century England. (French Deism, by contrast, was more radical.) A list of the tenets of classical Deism, written in the mid-1600s by the so-called father of English Deism, Lord Herbert of Cherbury, summarized it this way: "[God] had implanted in the human soul in the beginning five innate religious ideas: the existence of God, divine worship, the practice of virtue, repentance for sin, and personal immortality."[1] Deists distrusted, and some loudly denounced, such things as scripture, clergy, tradition, miracles and the like—anything that involved the claim that God had intervened in the world after He was finished creating it. The Deist movement initially grew popular in the colonies. But it soon peaked before largely dying out by early in the nineteenth century. Deism gained ground as the sciences experienced tremendous growth. Not long after Lord Herbert, Isaac Newton introduced his theories of physics, which proclaimed that careful observation of the physical world allows man to discover "insurmountable and uniform natural laws" that can be stated with mathematical precision.[2]

A WATCHMAKER?

As we saw earlier, Newton essentially held that the beauty and order of the universe implied that it was the work of a Creator. The Deists agreed—and wondered aloud if we really needed anything beyond our natural reason to understand a Creator who was, in their view, apparently uninvolved with His creation ever since, though He nevertheless could be counted on to bestow rewards and mete out punishments in the hereafter.

It is important not to overstate Deism's significance. First, full-throated Deists were not as numerous as some suppose. According to the late Jesuit scholar Avery Dulles, of the fifty-six signers of the Declaration of Independence, the theological leanings of some twenty have been identified.[3] Three were Deists and quasi-Deists. There were six liberal Christians, two of whom displayed Deist influences, and eleven more or less orthodox Christians.[4]

Second, Deists in America were typically doctrinally more flexible than their European coreligionists. They were, for example, somewhat more open to the notion of God's providence—and especially his care for the colonists—than was the more doctrinaire version predominant in Europe. In his autobiography, Benjamin Franklin discusses his youthful conversion from being a Presbyterian dissenter to "a thorough Deist."[5] As he goes on recounting his life's journey, he notes that "Revelation indeed had no weight" with him.[6] And yet as he relates all this, he credits "Providence" with guiding him. He manifested the same confidence in Providence's favor on America. When he took the floor at the Constitutional Convention, Franklin chastised his colleagues for their ingratitude to their "powerful friend" who had manifestly aided them during the Revolution:

> In this situation of this Assembly, groping as it were in the dark to find political truth, and scarce able to distinguish it when presented to us, how has it happened, Sir, that we have not hitherto once thought of humbly applying to the Father of lights to illuminate our understandings? In the beginnings of the contest with G. Britain, when we were sensible of danger we had daily prayer in this room for the divine protection.—Our prayers, Sir, were heard, and they were graciously answered. All of us who were engaged in the struggle must

have observed frequent instances of a superintending providence in our favor. To that kind providence we owe this happy opportunity of consulting in peace on the means of establishing our future national felicity. And have we now forgotten that powerful friend? Or do we imagine that we no longer need his assistance? I have lived, Sir, a long time, and the longer I live, the more convincing proofs I see of this truth—*that God governs in the affairs of men.*[7]

This passage is widely quoted as a historical precedent in support of public prayer. But examples of public prayer among the Founders are a dime a dozen. What is truly interesting here is what Franklin is urging them to pray for, that the "Father of lights . . . illuminate our understandings" in order "to find political truths." Moreover, he urges them on to confidence by reminding them that their earlier prayers during the Revolution had been "heard, and they were graciously answered." He concludes, "The longer I live, the more convincing proofs I see of this truth—*that God governs in the affairs of men*" (emphasis in the original). Now, his argument for God governing human affairs is an argument from experience, not from theology. Nevertheless, this would not appear to be the prayer of a "thorough Deist," at least not in the purist European sense of that term. Franklin, it seems, just wasn't given to orthodoxy, even in his heresies.

There were many shades of Deism, ranging from Thomas Paine's version, which was just this side of atheism, to that of Deist-tinged Christians like John Adams. And there was as much religious acrimony between the hard-core Deists and traditional Christians as there was among believers from other faiths. In his pamphlet entitled "Of the Religion of Deism Compared with the Christian Religion," Thomas Paine wrote of the Apostles' Creed: "The truth of the first article [of the Creed] is proved by God Himself, and is universal; for the creation is of itself demonstration of the existence of a Creator. But the second article, that of God's begetting a son, is not proved in like manner, and stands on no other authority than that of a tale."

Jefferson was more discreet than Paine and had better political sense than to publish his religious views at all, much less in a pamphlet. Nevertheless, he held a similar view of the Incarnation. Writing privately to John Adams: "And the day will come when the mystical generation of Jesus, by the Supreme Being as his father in the womb of a virgin will be classed with the fable of the generation of Minerva in the brain of Jupiter."[8]

We noted earlier that Jefferson said he had written the Declaration in such a way as to capture "the harmonizing sentiments of the day." That wouldn't be even his version of Deism. No, Deism was one of the individual strains that required harmonizing. The idea that Deists had in common with the more or less orthodox Christians was a philosophical theism.

An Alliance of Theists

So what's the difference? Deism is a *religion* that teaches that all that can be known about God by reason alone is all that can be known about Him, period. He does not reveal Himself. It's also all that's worth knowing about God because He won't be involved in your life. Likewise, there's little point in praying for God's interventions. Even the somewhat more muscular version of Deism that Franklin found agreeable, which made some room for Providence, still featured a very aloof and limited God. Deism was not a catchall, lowest-common-denominator idea. Quite the contrary, it was a particular and not especially spacious religion.

Philosophical theism, on the other hand, had—and has—no such limits. It is a *philosophy* that holds that there is a God who is one, who is good, who is just, and who—unlike the Deist deity—may very well be much more besides. Those few attributes we just listed may be about all that reason itself can demonstrate. But theism does not preclude God from revealing more of Himself. It just holds that the content of any such revelations would exceed reason's ability to discover on its own. Theism is a broad conceptual category, an umbrella that makes room for Judaism, Christianity, Islam, and so on—as well as for Deism itself. George Washington is a good example. As philosopher Michael Novak has pointed out, Washington's faith was more or less orthodox. But when he spoke publicly, he generally used the language of theism.[9]

As we've seen, ever since Aristotle introduced his Unmoved Mover, and ever since the Apostle Paul wrote to the Romans and preached in Athens, thinkers and believers have agreed on something very important. They have agreed that God's existence and some of His attributes can be known by human reason alone. What's more, they have agreed that other, very important things about God cannot. Simply put, human reason by itself can lead us to conclude there is a God. But it can't tell us who He is. Only He can do that.

That consensus continued among thinkers and thoughtful believers up through the Enlightenment to the time of our founding (and it remains an intellectually respectable position today). It was part of the curriculum in the colleges and universities and the premise of the Founders' political philosophy. It is not an overstatement to say that the Revolution was an alliance of theists—orthodox believers joining forces with radical Deists on the basis not of either one's theology but of their common intellectual heritage of theism.

James Madison and Thomas Jefferson are good examples of why that matters. "Nature's God," in the words of the Declaration, is the God that both men were convinced existed. But that wasn't because of Madison's more or less orthodox Christian faith. Nor was it due to Jefferson's lack of one. It was because Madison and Jefferson both thought God's existence was rationally self-evident. Madison believed this same God, whose existence he was rationally convinced of, had revealed himself much more fully in Jesus of

Nazareth. Jefferson didn't quite. But even as profound a disagreement as that did not keep them (or for that matter, Samuel Adams and Thomas Paine, who were even further apart theologically) from agreeing on the philosophy behind America's bid for independence. As profound as their theological divide over the hereafter may have been, their philosophical agreement about the here-and-now was truly momentous.

CHAPTER TEN

The Later Life of a Nation Under God

A s we've seen, at the time of the founding, there was a long and distinguished tradition stretching back all the way to Aristotle and Cicero for rationally investigating the possibility that God exists. There was likewise much reflection on the implication His existence would have for the just limits on our governance. The Founders stood firmly in that tradition. Giants standing on the shoulders of giants, they brought about something strikingly new: the American experiment.

The premise of their argument was that we were not merely subjects of a distant monarch but individuals who were fundamentally equal to that monarch, with inalienable rights that even the king must respect. What's more, they had this equality and possessed these rights not from some sort of royal entitlement or grant but as nothing less than a gift from God. We were not only born equal; we were created equal. We were not merely granted rights; we were "endowed" with them by our "Creator" Himself.

And which favored faith did one have to profess to enjoy the legal and political benefits of these ideas? Why, none at all. Well then, to whose idea of God must one subscribe in order to get them? Again, none at all. The whole point was not what an individual citizen professed. It was what the *government* acknowledged.

It was "self-evident" that all this was so. Why? Because it had been arguably "self-evident" at least since Aristotle that a God was so. To repeat, one need not profess any particular creed or even have faith at all. In order to claim the benefits of the argument that we were created equal and had inalienable rights, it was sufficient merely that the *government* acknowledge what was then a commonplace: it was evident from reason alone that there existed a God who was one, good, and just, and who would reward good and punish evil. Nobody needed to believe or think anything. The government just had to acknowledge philosophical theism.

ALIVE AND WELL

Happily, both of the big ideas that undergird our rights have been embraced by American governments and the overwhelming majority of the American people ever since. They are alive and well today.

It is still intellectually respectable to say that one can come to know that God exists, and a few basic things about Him, from reason alone. The argument on both sides has, of course, become increasingly sophisticated. The physicist Dr. John Polkinghorne, for example, continues his tireless research to explore the relationship among physics, metaphysics, and religion, with over two dozen books on the topic. Joining him are notable theist scientists such as Stephen Barr, Owen Gingerich, Peter Hodgson, Michal Heller, and Marco Bersanelli, among others.

Not everyone is in agreement, of course. Stephen Hawking, for instance, closes his book *The Grand Design* with a bold assertion refuting any such nonsense as a Creator: "Spontaneous creation is the reason there is something rather than nothing, why the universe exists, why we exist. It is not necessary to invoke God to light the blue touch paper and set the universe going."[1] But then, not everyone need agree on the Philosophers' God. That's the beauty of inalienable natural rights.

The philosophical question of God has continued a long run of respectability since the early days of the United States. So, too, the practical application of being a country "under God" has played a vital role in sorting through some of the thorniest civil and political challenges we have faced as a nation in the generations since.

UNDER GOD AT GETTYSBURG

Slavery's most implacable foe was the Philosophers' God. The abolitionist movement was premised on the idea that slaves, like all human beings, had rights bestowed by God, and that the government, and even the positive law of the Constitution, had no right to take them away.

In 1785, Alexander Hamilton helped found the nation's first abolitionist society, the New York Society for Promoting the Manumission of Slaves. At its opening meeting, the following statement was read: "The benevolent Creator and Father of men, having given to them all an equal right to life, liberty, and property, no Sovereign power on earth can justly deprive them of either."[2]

A celebrated case involving a man charged with violating the Fugitive Slave Act is a good illustration. Lawyer and future Chief Justice Salmon P. Chase defended his client, John Van Zandt, by arguing that "the law of the Creator, which invests every human being with an inalienable title to freedom, cannot be repealed by any [human] law which asserts that man is property."[3]

And as the fault line of slavery threatened to fracture the union, it would be a former representative from Illinois who would do the most, by deed and by word, to reunite the country. President Abraham Lincoln would pay the ultimate price for his commitment to ending slavery in America. But it's the words by which he did so, and his use of one phrase in particular, is especially remarkable.

In the fields of Pennsylvania, on a sunny November day in 1863, the Honorable Edward Everett was slated as the main attraction at the dedication of what would henceforth be a national cemetery for the soldiers who fought and died in one of the Civil War's bloodiest battles. Everett was a celebrated orator. And orate he did—for nearly two hours. The crowd received the remarks well enough. And then forgot them in short order.

The next guest spoke for all of two minutes. But in ten sentences, President Lincoln's Gettysburg Address managed to completely eclipse Everett's speech. Nobody remembers a word from Everett. Lincoln's speech, by contrast, is still read by every schoolchild and remembered as one of the best speeches ever delivered.[4]

Lincoln's Gettysburg Address is remarkable for another, lesser known reason: it's one of the very few times Lincoln changed a speech on the fly. Lincoln was a deliberate speaker and rarely wavered from his carefully prepared texts. In the case of his address at Gettysburg, we know Lincoln wrote at least two drafts before, and produced three additional copies after his speech. There are slight stylistic differences between the five versions. But most notably, the three later copies share in common the addition of two words not found in the first two drafts of Lincoln's text.

Both the Bancroft copy (named after noted historian George Bancroft, who requested the additional copy from Lincoln) and the Bliss copy (the only version to which Lincoln attached his signature), along with the version now carved on the walls of the Lincoln Memorial in Washington, D.C., conclude: "that this nation *under God* shall have a new birth of freedom, and that government of the people, by the people, for the people, shall not perish from the earth."[5] The words *under God* don't appear in the two drafts prepared in advance.

Perhaps it was the solemnity of the grounds he stood on that inspired Lincoln to feel compelled to include this rare ad-lib, but he almost certainly did not conjure up the phrase on his own. A serious student of history and political theory, Lincoln must have been well aware of the history and use of *under God* in the Western political and legal tradition we explored earlier, from Washington's statements and Coke's opinion all the way through abolitionist arguments. Lincoln's invocation was a continuation of that tradition: an appeal not to a specific theological doctrine but to a particular political philosophy rooted in natural rights and the Philosophers' God.

ONE NATION, UNDER GOD,
INDIVISIBLE

I t's no coincidence that the journey of President Lincoln's famous ad-lib into the Pledge of Allegiance began on his birthday and in his home state. On February 12, 1948, the Society of the Sons of the American Revolution gathered in Chicago to celebrate Lincoln's birthday. To mark the occasion in honor of the Great Emancipator, the society amended its opening recitation of the Pledge by inserting the phrase *under God*—an idea credited to society chaplain Louis A. Bowman.

By 1951 the "under God" movement started to gain steam nationwide with the help of the Knights of Columbus, the largest fraternal Catholic organization in the world. In April 1951 "the Board of Directors of the Knights of Columbus adopted a resolution to amend the Pledge of Allegiance as recited" at all of the nearly eight hundred of the Fourth, or highest, Degree assembly meetings.[6] The next year they passed a similar resolution requiring the change in wording at all group meetings and began petitioning the president, the vice president, and members of Congress that the change be made universal. Following the Knights of Columbus' next round of petitioning in 1953, seventeen resolutions had been introduced into the House of Representatives to officially amend the Pledge.

Shortly thereafter, on February 7, 1954, President Eisenhower heard a memorable sermon by Reverend George MacPherson Docherty at the New York Avenue Presbyterian Church—a church President Lincoln had sometimes attended. The church commemorated that history with a traditional "Lincoln pew," which, on that day, was occupied by President Eisenhower.

With an eye toward the growing conflict between the United States and Soviet Russia, Docherty delivered a rousing sermon on the Pledge and his growing concern that something about it wasn't quite right:

There was something missing in the Pledge, and that which was missing was the characteristic and definitive factor in the "American Way of Life." Indeed, apart from the mention of the phrase, the United States of America, this could be the Pledge of *any* Republic. In fact, I could hear little Muscovites repeat a similar pledge to their hammer and sickle flag in Moscow with equal solemnity, for Russia is also a Republic that claims to have overthrown the tyranny of kingship.

Then, drawing upon Lincoln's ad-lib at Gettysburg, Docherty submitted his recommendation for an addition to the Pledge that would sufficiently distinguish it from the Soviets:

"One nation UNDER GOD" this people shall know a new birth of freedom, and *UNDER GOD* are the definitive words. . . . We face, today, a theological war. . . . To omit the words "Under God" in the Pledge of Allegiance is to omit the definitive character of the "American Way of Life."[7]

With the support of Eisenhower, Docherty's sermon spread rapidly across the country and through the halls of Congress: "Four months later the resolution introduced by Congressman Louis C. Rabaut of Michigan, and supported by the Knights of Columbus, was adopted by both houses of Congress and signed by President Dwight D. Eisenhower on Flag Day, June 14, 1954."[8]

In a letter following the action, President Eisenhower thanked Supreme Knight Luke Hart for the Knights of Columbus' work in making the addition of the words *under God* to the Pledge a reality:

> I am happy to send greetings to the Knights of Columbus on the occasion of the annual meeting of your Supreme Council. . . . And this year we are particularly thankful to you for your part in the movement to have the

words "under God" added to our Pledge of Allegiance. These words will remind Americans that despite our great physical strength we must remain humble. They will help us to keep constantly in our minds and hearts the spiritual and moral principles which alone give dignity to man, and upon which our way of life is founded.[9]

Now, people of different religious and political persuasions tell that story for different purposes. One side tells it to point out how there was precedent for the addition of *under God* as an enunciation of the "American way of life" and as distinct from the Soviets. Others tell the story this way: "Look at how those religious folks in the funny hats were able to push their God into the Pledge."

To be sure, most of those who led the charge to add *under God* were religious believers of one type or another. But while Reverend Docherty was right to say that what differentiated the "American way of life" from that of the Russians was a "battle of the gods," he was in an important respect mistaken. At its core the war was philosophical, not theological.

As the House report explained, Congress added those words with the express purpose of textually rejecting the "communist" philosophy "with its attendant subservience of the individual":

> At this moment of our history the principles underlying our American Government and the American way of life are under attack by a system whose philosophy is at direct odds with our own. Our American Government is founded on the concept of the individuality and the dignity of the human being. Underlying this concept is the belief that the human person is important because he was created by God and endowed by Him with certain inalienable rights which no civil authority may usurp. The inclusion of God in our pledge therefore would further acknowledge the dependence of our people and our Government upon the

moral directions of the Creator. At the same time it would serve to deny the atheistic and materialistic concepts of communism with its attendant subservience of the individual.[10]

The House report also quotes from other proponents of the political philosophy of natural rights. William Penn, for example, had said, "'Those people who are not governed by God will be ruled by tyrants.'"[11] And George Mason had explained, "'All acts of legislature apparently contrary to the natural right and justice are, in our laws, and must be in the nature of things considered as void. The laws of nature are the laws of God, whose authority can be superseded by no power on earth.'"[12]

Soviet legal theory, by contrast, had rejected the philosophy of natural rights, maintaining that all rights are derived from the state: "Natural law doctrine is rejected. There are no civil rights derived from sources other than positive law. As positive law is created by the state, all civil rights are to be granted by the state."[13]

The legislative history of *under God* is replete with references to "times such as these,"[14] "communism,"[15] "the conflict now facing us,"[16] "a time in the world,"[17] and "this moment in history."[18] Individual legislators repeatedly argued for the phrase *under God* as an express rejection of Communist political philosophy and a reaffirmation of American political philosophy.[19]

This was not some jingoistic exercise in contrasting good believers with bad atheists. It was a serious reflection on the different philosophical visions of human nature—and therefore of human freedom—that underlay the two systems.

When Congress reenacted the Pledge in 2002, its references to the political philosophy of natural rights were just as prominent. Congress made numerous findings grounding the Pledge on the idea of "Laws of Nature, and of Nature's God," and the idea that people "are endowed by their Creator with certain unalienable Rights."[20] As the Ninth Circuit would later conclude:

These findings make it absolutely clear that Congress in 2002 was not trying to impress a religious doctrine upon anyone. Rather, they had two main purposes for keeping the phrase "one Nation under God" in the Pledge: (1) to underscore the political philosophy of the Founding Fathers that God granted certain inalienable rights to the people which the government cannot take away; and (2) to add the note of importance which a Pledge to our Nation ought to have and which in our culture ceremonial references to God arouse.[21]

In short, when Congress amended the Pledge in 1954 and reaffirmed it in 2002, it was expressly drawing on the political philosophy of the Founders, embodied most prominently in the Declaration of Independence. It contended simply that people who live under a government that recognizes a higher power than itself live in greater freedom. By adopting the phrase *under God* in the Pledge, Congress brought it within the "natural rights" philosophy of Washington, Hamilton, Jefferson, Madison, and Lincoln—the philosophy on which the American system is based—and rejected the Soviet view that all rights are conferred at the pleasure of the State.

CHAPTER ELEVEN

A Nation Under God: Some FAQs

N ow, what real difference would all this make? Isn't this just some academic's pet theory, perfect for starting an argument in the faculty lounge but, practically speaking, completely inert? What if you disagree with it? And whatever happened to the separation of church and state? Good questions, all. Let's take the last question first.

SEPARATION OF CHURCH AND
STATE: LESSONS IN SHORTHAND

As it's used in constitutional law, *separation of church and state* is a shorthand phrase, much like *separation of powers*. Neither phrase actually appears in the Constitution itself. Rather, each is shorthand for a collection of specific provisions that do. The phrase *separation of powers* refers to the structural principle colloquially known as the "system of checks and balances." It's there for the express purpose of making political life difficult. The Framers saw that a good way of protecting the nation against lapsing into tyranny would be to prevent anybody in the government from being able to accomplish too much too easily. So they divided the government's authority among three distinct branches—the legislative, the executive, and the judicial—and then gave each branch vested institutional interests that were at odds with the others.

For example, in order to become a federal judge, that is, to become an official of the *judicial* branch, one has to be nominated by the president (the head of the *executive* branch), and be confirmed by the Senate (in the *legislative* branch). Likewise, only the Congress can declare war, but only the president (who is commander in chief) can prosecute a war.

Separation of powers thus is shorthand for Article I, section 1; Article II, section 1; and Article III, section 1 of the Constitution. Those provisions broadly provide that the legislative power, the executive power, and the judicial power are vested in Congress, the president, and the courts, respectively.

Simple enough, so far. But *separation of powers* is also shorthand for other, more counterintuitive provisions found in the Constitution. The Appointments Clause, for example, empowers the president "by and with the advice and consent of the Senate" to appoint ambassadors, prosecutors, and the like. But it also includes an important exception: "the Congress may by Law vest the appointment of such inferior Officers, as they think proper, in the president alone, *in the*

Courts of Law [emphasis added], or in the Heads of Departments."[1] That is to say, while the Constitution generally vests the executive power in the president, here it makes an exception. In the Appointments Clause it takes a small piece of the executive power—the authority to appoint some inferior officers of the United States—and allows Congress to assign that authority to the "courts of law," that is, the judicial branch.

Similarly, the Impeachment Clause assigns some of the judicial power, which would normally belong to the courts, to the Senate instead, and the Veto Clause assigns a bit of legislative power, which would ordinarily belong to Congress, to the president.[2] Now, unless you understand that these provisions exist and are also encompassed in the shorthand phrase *separation of powers,* you will soon run into trouble. That is, if you try to give the phrase *separation of powers* a legal force all its own—rather than using it as only shorthand for the constitutional provisions that really do have legal force—you will misunderstand the law in various important respects.

In other words, *separation of powers* is perfectly good shorthand—provided you remember that it's shorthand. Otherwise, it's an outright obstacle to properly understanding the Constitution.

The same is true of *separation of church and state*. That phrase doesn't appear in the Constitution, either. Once again, though, it's very serviceable shorthand for other provisions that do—*so long as you remember that it's shorthand.*[3]

For the most part, *separation of church and state* refers to the Establishment Clause ("Congress shall make no law respecting an establishment of religion") and the Free Exercise Clause ("or prohibiting the free exercise thereof") of the First Amendment. But it also stands for the Oaths Clause, the No Religious Test Clause, certain aspects of the Free Speech Clause, the Equal Protection Clause, and so on. And just as was the case with *separation of powers,* if all you know of *separation of church and state* is the shorthand phrase itself, and not what it's shorthand for, you will go seriously astray.

So then, what's the full meaning of *separation of church and state*? And why doesn't government acknowledgment of a Creator violate it?

The Bad Old Days

S ome historical and legal context: We are so used to enjoying our freedom of speech, freedom of the press, freedom of religion, and so forth that it is difficult for us to grasp that there was a time when these freedoms, and the others secured by the Bill of Rights, did not even exist with respect to state law. It seems all but impossible to us: how utterly un-American for a state to be able to persecute its citizens for saying the wrong thing, publishing the wrong thing, or following the wrong religion. How could that ever have been the law? Surely the Constitution has always protected people's rights from infringement by their state governments, hasn't it?

Actually, as unthinkable as it now seems, from the ratification of the Constitution until at least the end of the Civil War, states were perfectly free, at least as a matter of federal law, to outlaw their citizens' speech, publishing, religious expression, and so on. Now, individual states could, and sometimes did, at least partially secure those rights in *state* constitutions and law. More often they did very little to protect people's rights. And federal law was all but useless.

In 1842, for example, Father Bernard Permoli, a Roman Catholic priest in New Orleans, was fined fifty dollars for violating a city ordinance that prohibited corpses from being displayed in public during funeral rites. Father Permoli resisted the fine, claiming that the ordinance violated his First Amendment right to free exercise of religion. The Supreme Court rejected that argument out of hand: "The Constitution makes no provision for protecting the citizens of the respective states in their religious liberties; this is left to the state constitutions and laws; nor is there any inhibition imposed by the Constitution of the United States."[4] That the Bill of Rights did not originally apply to the states is thus not at all a controversial statement. Nobody seriously disputes it. It is simply a historical fact.

Now, it is not a happy fact, to be sure. Those were not the "good old days" to which we should all hearken back. However, it's important to see this history for what it was. Some of the Framers, notably James Madison, wanted from the beginning for the Bill of Rights to protect the citizenry from state law incursions as much as it did from federal ones. And subsequent history would demonstrate that Madison and his friends had been prescient. They simply lacked the votes to accomplish their objective. The political realities were otherwise.

Eleven of the thirteen states represented at the Constitutional Convention—all but Virginia and New York—imposed at least some religious test for state and local officeholders. Some actually had full-blown religious establishments. Massachusetts, for example, had a tax-supported, legally established Congregationalist faith—and would go on to keep it until 1833.[5] Other states, Vermont for instance, didn't quite have an official faith but nonetheless required all would-be candidates for public office to "own and profess the Protestant religion."[6] So even while proclaiming loudly that everyone had a natural right to religious freedom, the majority of delegates to the Constitutional Convention were in favor of restricting only *federal* law on the question of religion. They wanted to leave states free to regulate it as they saw fit.

We see this juxtaposition codified in the Oaths Clause and the No Religious Test Clause of Article VI, section 3 of the Constitution. The Oaths Clause provides that officeholders "both of the United States and of the several States" would be "bound by Oath *or Affirmation*" to support the Constitution (emphasis added). It's then followed by the provision that "no religious Test shall ever be required as a Qualification to any Office or public Trust *under the United States*" (emphasis added). Read together, those two clauses demonstrate that *both* federal and state officeholders were protected from having to be sworn in to office and could simply affirm their dedication, Quaker style. But only *federal* officials were protected from religious tests for office. State officials were not. Why the difference? Political reality. Since the majority of the states had their own religious requirements for public office—and wanted to keep them—there simply were not enough votes to extend that protection to state officials.

Even when the Bill of Rights was finally proposed by Congress in 1789 and ratified by the States shortly thereafter, it did nothing to upset the status quo on the question of religion. Political realities had not changed. If anything, the Bill of Rights etched the status quo more deeply into the law. Despite Madison's best efforts, it provided only that the federal government could not interfere with religion in state law, either by imposing a federally established religion on states (such as Virginia, which had none), or by using a federal *disestablishment* to override state-established religions (in places like Massachusetts). Being explicitly disabled from doing either of those things, Congress could thus "make no law respecting an establishment of religion."

Nor could Congress single out a particular faith for legal *disfavor*—as Vermont had done for Catholics, Jews, and others, and as virtually every state had done at one time or another to Quakers. Congress could thus "make no law . . . prohibiting the free exercise" of religion. The states, though, could—and did—make any such laws they chose.

FIRST AMENDMENT, INC.

And there matters stood, until the advent of the Fourteenth Amendment in the wake of the Civil War. That amendment was later interpreted by the Supreme Court to make many provisions of the Bill of Rights, including the Establishment and Free Exercise Clauses, applicable to the states. The Court announced that they had been "incorporated" into the word *liberty* in the Fourteenth Amendment's Due Process Clause.

That incorporation has turned out to be easier said than done—particularly with respect to the Establishment Clause, which has its own peculiar wording. The Supreme Court has been trying to sort out just what it might mean ever since.

To repeat, the era in which states could—and did—legally persecute their citizens for their exercise of their religion was in no way, shape, or form, a golden age of American history for which we should be nostalgic. It was, rather, a mistake to be learned from and not repeated. Nevertheless, for all its warts, the history of the Constitution demonstrates clearly how unthinkable it would've been for anyone to claim with a straight face that the First Amendment somehow prohibited public recitation of the Declaration of Independence or any of the broad array of other documents referring to God as the ultimate source of our rights. Recall, too, that even Virginia, which was the leading state opting for disestablishment, explicitly premised its disestablishment on the natural right to religious freedom: "We are free to declare, and do declare, that the rights hereby asserted are of the natural rights of mankind, and that if any act shall be hereafter passed to repeal the present, or to narrow its operation, such act will be an infringement of natural right."[7]

And lest there be any doubt, that statute took pains to emphasize the premise of those natural rights themselves. They followed, it said, from the fact that "Almighty God hath created the mind free."

A GROWING CONSENSUS

What about more recent precedents? As of this writing, the Supreme Court has not ruled on the merits of a challenge to *under God* in the Pledge of Allegiance, and none appears on the horizon. A broad array of individual Justices over several decades, however, have—on one rationale or another—referred approvingly to *under God* in the Pledge in their opinions. Now,

some of these rationales have been more satis-
factory than others. (As we saw earlier, the late
Justice William Brennan's and retired justice Sandra Day O'Connor's invocation of "ceremonial
deism," for example, are particularly dubious.)
Nevertheless, as one federal appellate judge observes, it is "noteworthy that, given the vast number of Establishment Clause cases to come before
the Court, *not one Justice has ever suggested
that the Pledge is unconstitutional.* In an area of
law sometimes marked by befuddlement and lack
of agreement, such unanimity is striking."[8]

All told, following Dr. Newdow's losses (and
the Becket Fund's wins) in the First and Ninth
Circuits, any reasonable handicapper would set
the odds of a successful challenge to *under God*
as very long.

WHAT IF YOU DISAGREE?

S elf-evident" to whom? What if you think that there is nothing out there, not even the Philosophers' God? That America's political philosophy is mistaken? That Nature itself doesn't exist? In short, what if the notion that we are "endowed" by our "Creator" with "unalienable rights" is not at all "self-evident" to you? What then? Do you still have the same rights as everybody else?

Yes, of course. Your rights do not follow from your holding certain opinions; they follow from who you are. Nobody has to believe in anything. We don't have to think anything, or profess anything either, in order to enjoy our natural rights. It's the *government* that has to recognize something—that it must respect our rights because they come from a source higher than, and prior to, it. We need only hold the government to its word. As a practical matter, that would be true no matter what theory of rights dissidents embrace—other dissidents would presumably claim the right to dissent from it.

More fundamentally, everyone is fully entitled to dissent from the ideas in the Declaration of Independence, the Pledge of Allegiance, or anything else for that matter, and to refuse to recite them. As we saw in Chapter 2, the Supreme Court settled that long ago in the *Barnette* case. Under *Barnette,* conscientious objectors have the free speech and free exercise rights not to be coerced into reciting something that they don't believe is true. They may discreetly step out of the room, they may respectfully remain seated, they may stand and be silent, or they may omit the offending words, *under God,* from their recitation of the Pledge. They may do anything their consciences dictate they must, as long as it is not disruptive of the rights of others.

What they are not entitled to do, however, is to enlist the Establishment Clause to prevent other willing participants from reciting them. The Establishment Clause is not implicated by their dissent from *under God* in the Pledge any more than it would be by their dissent from the principle we are a nation that is "indivisible." True, one phrase includes the word *God* and the other does not, but both are philosophical assertions, not religious ones. And the Establishment Clause is not at issue when the government is simply making philosophical claims.

WHAT DIFFERENCE WOULD IT MAKE?

Even leaving aside the intrinsic advantages of thinking straight, the Philosophers' God comes with practical advantages as well. It makes a very big difference in the shape of our rights and how we can assert them. It makes a difference as well in how the government conducts itself and what it can demand of us.

Not all problems require judicial solutions or even constitutional ones. We have a long and distinguished tradition of Congress and state legislatures respecting individuals' consciences in a wide variety of contexts. Thus federal law exempts conscientious objectors from serving in combat, from taking oaths in court, from serving on juries, and so on.

This tradition makes the best sense in the context of natural rights. The Constitution, while it secures much protection for religious liberty, does not exhaust the natural right to religious liberty itself. This is another important insight from James Madison's thought. We've seen how he advanced natural rights theory. As for how those natural rights relate to legal ones, Madison believed the latter exist to secure the former. But he learned through hard experience that, given the nature of legislatures and political give-and-take, it was inevitable that legal rights would secure natural rights only imperfectly at best.

He had not come to this conclusion lightly. In fact, by his lights, the Constitution—or more precisely, we the people—would have been better off without a Bill of Rights at all. The Bill of Rights, Madison feared, could not realistically be expected to secure the full breadth of the rights it would enumerate. He thought it far better to argue under the full expanse of the natural rights to freedom of religion, freedom of speech, and the like, rather than risk a narrow interpretation of constitutional language itself resulting in a greatly restricted set of rights.

Jefferson persuaded him, with the help of some influential state legislators, of the notion that "Half a loaf is better than no bread. If we cannot secure all our rights, let us secure what we can."[9] What then of the natural rights under a constitutional framework? Madison was emphatic: the Bill of Rights does not secure all the individual rights there are. On the contrary, both in the Virginia legislature—where he was battling a bill to publicly fund clergy—and later in life, while inveighing somewhat more quixotically against funding congressional chaplains, Madison did not hesitate to argue that some legislative actions that were permitted by the state or federal constitution nevertheless violated the natural right of religious liberty.

In his famous "Memorial and Remonstrance Against Religious Assessments," Madison found himself having to argue against the enactment of a bill that was clearly constitutional under state law, as measured by the religious freedom provision of the Virginia Declaration of Rights, the state analogue to the First Amendment. Madison knew all too well that the proposed statute would not run afoul of Virginia's constitution. He had served on the committee responsible for writing the Declaration of Rights and had attempted to outlaw government support for the established Anglican Church in Virginia, only to see that effort fail. To Madison's chagrin, the majority of the legislature, although happy to declare religious freedom a natural right, nevertheless had insisted on maintaining the privileges of the established church. Thus Madison knew, perhaps better than anyone, that the Virginia Declaration of Rights, which did not bar state funding of even one church, could not plausibly be read to bar the funding of all churches. The law was clearly against Madison's position. Nevertheless, in the "Memorial and Remonstrance," he gamely argued that the natural right to religious freedom prohibited such statutes. And he carried the day.

Similarly, in a less famous treatise written during his retirement and later dubbed his "Detached Memorandum," Madison argued that government funding of congressional chaplains was improper. He thought it should be held to violate the First Amendment (a position that even the modern Supreme Court has rejected). Failing that, he said, funding chaplains should be discontinued because it violated the "pure principle," or natural right, of religious liberty itself.[10] The point here is not whether Madison was right or wrong on chaplains, only that well after the First Amendment had become law, Madison saw no problem with measuring a particular governmental action against the "pure principle" of religious freedom.

And neither should we. We should take Madison up on his insight and insist on our natural right to religious freedom even where it is outside the protection of written law. This does not mean urging on the federal courts' extraconstitutional bases for their decisions. It does mean, however, that other branches and levels of government may take into account legitimate claims for the natural right of religious liberty in making their own decisions.

How would that work? Let's take an example from a hypothetical case in a state court. A frequently heard criticism of the Supreme Court's current free exercise doctrine is that it's so narrow it wouldn't even protect a first-communion class from being raided by local authorities for underage drinking. And perhaps that's so. But if a local district attorney should foolishly seek to prosecute children on that basis, other government entities could ride to the rescue under the natural right to religious liberty. The members of the grand jury, for example, could and should refuse to indict. The trial jurors in the case could and should refuse to convict in any case that made it that far. The governor could and should pardon the children and their parents and make clear his intent to pardon anybody else convicted under such a ridiculous interpretation of the law. And in all events, the local legislators could and should intervene in the nonsense, by passing legislative exemptions for underage sipping of communion wine and by impeaching the prosecutor.[11]

Not all appeals to conscience are so dramatic, however. Far from it. Most are as mundane as a city council scheduling its meetings around religious holidays. Or the local library making an unwritten exception to its no-hats-indoors policy for someone's yarmulke. And so on. Such appeals to, and respect for, conscience happen all the time. Which is much of the point: natural rights come naturally.

CHAPTER TWELVE

A Conundrum Revisited

Newdow's Conundrum, you'll recall, was "If you can't lead public school children in reciting 'one nation under Jesus,' how can you lead them in pledging allegiance to 'one nation under God'?" It was a dilemma that posed a challenge to the entire American rights tradition. Our tradition is that we are all equal and possessed of inalienable rights because the Creator has made it so. It's "self-evident" that this is the case. But if Newdow were correct, then it would now be unthinkable to say that the Creator had done any such thing. What, if anything, would ground our rights? What would ground our equality? And even beyond both of those perhaps abstract-sounding questions, what would happen to our day-to-day consensus as Americans that not only are we equal to others, and have rights that we may enforce, but so do they?

We've traced the intellectual tradition—beginning with Aristotle and continuing to the present day—that concludes that the question of whether God "is" can be a philosophical question and not a religious one. Along the way, we bumped into the Being whose existence this tradition says it can prove. We dubbed him the Philosophers' God. Actually, we didn't quite meet him, we spotted him at a distance. Because it turns out, you can't really meet the Philosophers' God as such. Unlike the God as He is worshipped by various faith traditions, the Philosophers' God is not at all approachable. There is no First Church of the Philosophers' God, no hospitals and orphanages dedicated to him, no clergy claiming to speak on his behalf, and (on a brighter note) no collections taken up to pay for his shrines. The

Philosophers' God is the sum total of what can be known about God from reason alone.

This does not, though, make the Philosophers' God somehow a God-of-all-faiths, a lowest-common-denominator in the sky. His profile is not arrived at the way a greeting card's message is: by comparing all the various religions' teachings, then drafting a bland platitude they'll all buy. Rather, it's drawn from centuries of painstaking philosophical investigation.

Nor is the Philosophers' God a "different God" from the God of believers' faith. He is not some sort of idol or golden calf. But he's also not the fullness of the one God as believed in by, say, Abraham, Isaac, and Jacob. He is only as much of the one God as can be known by Aristotle, Einstein, and Jefferson.

As Lincoln famously declared in his Gettysburg Address, America was "conceived in Liberty" and dedicated to a *"proposition,"* namely, "that all . . . are created equal." Every American, in other words, is a bit of a philosopher, because our freedom is built on the foundation of certain philosophical propositions. Besides the proposition that we are created equal, Lincoln also stressed at Gettysburg the proposition that this nation is "under God." Neither Lincoln nor those who followed his lead in adding *under God* to the Pledge were composing a prayer or giving a theology lesson. They were simply affirming a truth that's part of the bedrock of America's political philosophy.

But isn't it a pity that so little can be said about the Philosophers' God? Wouldn't it be far better if we could just call the Creator by his true name? No, actually, it wouldn't. The great beauty of the Philosophers' God is precisely that so much of him remains hidden from reason alone. The most that may traditionally be *known* about the Philosophers' God is that he exists, that he is the Creator, and that he is just and good. To ardent believers that may seem like pretty thin gruel. But for our purposes, it's plenty. It makes the existence of the Philosophers' God an intellectual proposition potent enough to ground our individual rights but nowhere near strong enough to ground any sort of theocracy. Just as important, those who are unconvinced of his existence are staking out only a philosophical, not a theological, disagreement. They are protected conscientious objectors in a country that secures the rights of all, not reviled infidels in some confessional state. Their right to dissent will be scrupulously respected by a government that acknowledges that everyone's rights—including those of dissenters—are ultimately grounded in the Philosophers' God.

And that is nearly perfect for our purposes. For it answers many of the thorniest questions we face, including what is no doubt Newdow's personal favorite:

Question:
    If you can't say "one nation under Jesus,"
    how can you say "one nation under God"?
Answer:
    Simple. You can't say "one nation under
    Jesus" because that is a religious assertion,

which the government may never make.
The second—"one nation under God"—is a
philosophical assertion, and the government
makes those all the time.

Chapter One: Newdow's Conundrum

1. *Elk Grove Unified School District v. Newdow,* 542 U.S. 1 (2004).
2. Ibid., official transcript of oral arguments, *Oyez,* http://www.oyez.org/cases/2000-2009/2003/2003_02_1624.
3. T. S. Eliot, *Murder in the Cathedral* (Harcourt, Brace & World, 1963), p. 44.
4. "One Father, Back in Court, Indefatigable," *New York Times,* September 19, 2005.
5. Arthur E. Sutherland, "Book Reviews," *Indiana Law Journal* 40 no. 1 (1964), 83, 86 n. 7 (quoting, from memory, Rostow's unpublished 1962 Meiklejohn Lecture at Brown University). Sutherland was reviewing Walter G. Katz, *Religion and American Constitutions* (Evanston, IL: Northwestern University Press, 1963).
6. *Lynch v. Donnelly,* 465 U.S. 668, 716 (1984).
7. Ibid., emphasis added, citations omitted.
8. *County of Allegheny v. ACLU,* 492 U.S. 573 (1989).

9. Davison M. Douglas, "Ceremonial Deism," in
   Encyclopedia of American Civil Liberties,
   ed. Paul Finkelman (New York: Routledge,
   2006), pp. 258–59.

Chapter Two: The Pilgrims Pledge
Their Allegiance . . .

1. The Gobitises' surname was actually spelled
   Gobitas but changed in court opinions due to a
   clerical error. In a wild coincidence, the Barnetts'
   surname was also misspelled in federal court
   records as Barnette. This chapter will use the
   Gobitis and Barnette spellings to avoid confusion.
2. Shawn Francis Peters, *Judging Jehovah's Witnesses:
   Religious Persecution and the Dawn of the Rights
   Revolution* (Lawrence: University Press of Kansas,
   2000), p. 27.
3. Billy Gobitis, *Letter to the Schoolboard*
   (November 5, 1935), in *The Right to Free Speech,*
   ed. Claudia Isner (New York: Rosen, 2001), p. 75.
4. Peters, *Judging Jehovah's Witnesses,* pp. 36–38.
5. Ibid., pp. 43–45.
6. *Minersville School District v. Gobitis,* 310 U.S. 586
   (1940).
7. John Q. Barrett, "Recollections of *West Virginia*

State Board of Education v. Barnette," *St. John's Law Review* 81, no. 4 (Fall 2007), p. 761.

8. Peters, *Judging Jehovah's Witnesses,* pp. 74–75.

9. "The Courage to Put God First," *Awake!* (July 22, 1993), p. 15. See also Peters, *Judging Jehovah's Witnesses,* p. 79; see also "Members of Sect Beaten in Two Cities," *New York Times* (September 21, 1948), describing attacks in Little Rock, Arkansas, and Klamath, Oregon.

10. Peters, *Judging Jehovah's Witnesses,* p. 245.

11. Ibid., pp. 90–92.

12. Barrett, "Recollections of *West Virginia State Board of Education,"* pp. 770–71.

13. "[W]e now believe [Gobitis] . . . was wrongly decided," they wrote. "Certainly our democratic form of government . . . has a high responsibility to accommodate itself to the religious view of minorities however unpopular and unorthodox those views may be." *Jones v. City of Opelika,* 316 U.S. 584, 623–24 (1942) (Murphy, J., dissenting).

14. See *Ex Parte Quirin,* 317 U.S. 1 (1942), authorizing the military trials and executions of the saboteurs.

15. Barrett, "Recollections of *West Virginia State Board of Education,"* p. 771.

16. *West Virginia State Board of Education v. Barnette,* 319 U.S. 624 (1943).

Chapter Three: . . . And the Park Rangers Pledge Theirs

1. Michael Newdow, speech upon presentation of "Freethinker of the Year," before the 25th annual convention of the Freedom from Religion Foundation, Westin Horton Plaza Hotel, San Diego, CA, November 22, 2002.
2. Michael Newdow, interview, "Litigant Explains Why He Brought Pledge Suit," *CNN Access,* June 26, 2002, http://edition.cnn.com/2002/ LAW/06/26/Newdow.cnna/.
3. *Newdow et al. v. Congress of the United States et al.,* No. 05-cv-00017 (U.S. Court for the Eastern District of California, 2011), brief, http://www .becketfund.org/wp-content/uploads/2011/06/ 06-01-06-Pledge-Opening-Brief-Final.pdf.
4. *Newdow v. Rio Linda Union School District,* No. 05-17257 (9th Cir., 2010).
5. The dissent, by circuit judge Stephen Reinhardt, can best be described as apoplectic. It went on for more than 200 pages, arguing that "no judge familiar with the history of the Pledge could in good conscience believe . . . that the words under God were inserted into the Pledge for any purpose other than an explicitly and predominantly religious one." Ibid.

Chapter Four: An Inescapable Question . . .

1. Blaise Pascal, *Pensées* (1669), Part 3, § 233.
2. The agnostic philosopher and former president of the Italian Senate Marcello Pera made a similar point: "To live as if God existed means to deny man that giddy feeling of omnipotence and absolute freedom which at first elates him and then depresses and degrades him. It means recognizing our finite condition and becoming aware of the ethical limitations of our actions." See Marcello Pera, *Why We Must Call Ourselves Christians* (New York: Encounter, 2011), pp. 59–60.
3. *The Federalist Papers,* No. 84 (1788).
4. Alexander Hamilton, "The Farmer Refuted" (February 23, 1775), in *Papers of Alexander Hamilton,* ed. Harold C. Syrett et al. (New York: Columbia University Press, 1961–79), pp. 1:86–89, 121–22, 135–36.
5. John Adams, Inaugural Address, March 4, 1797, in *The Presidents Speak: The Inaugural Addresses of the American Presidents from George Washington to George Walker Bush*, ed. David Newton Lott (M. Hunter & H. Hunter, 2002), pp. 10–15.
6. William Henry Harrison, Inaugural Address, March 4, 1841, ibid., pp. 81–82.

7. John F. Kennedy, Inaugural Address, January 20, 1961, ibid., p. 306.
8. Ronald Reagan, First Inaugural Address, January 20, 1981, ibid., pp. 340–44.
9. Abraham Lincoln, Second Inaugural Address, March 5, 1864, ibid., p. 102.
10. *McGowan v. Maryland,* 366 U.S. 420, 562 (1961).
11. *Zorach v. Clauson,* 343 U.S. 306, 313 (1952); *Lynch v. Donnelly,* 465 U.S. 668, 675 (1984); *Marsh v. Chambers,* 463 U.S. 783, 813 (1983); *Walz v. Tax Comm'n,* 397 U.S. 664, 672 (1970); *Abington Sch. Dist. v. Schempp,* 374 U.S. 203, 213 (1963).
12. *McCreary County v. American Civil Liberties Union of Kentucky,* 545 U.S. 03-1693 (2005) (Scalia, A., dissenting).
13. Constitution of the State of New York, http://www.dos.ny.gov/info/constitution.htm.
14. G. K. Chesterton, *What I Saw in America* (1922; reprint ed. New York: Da Capo Press, 1968), p. 7.
15. Ibid., p. 10.

Chapter Five: . . . With a Great Deal at Stake in the Answer

1. "Religion: Santayana's Testament," *Time,* March 25, 1946.

2. Paul Mariani, *Lost Puritan: A Life of Robert Lowell* (New York: Norton, 1994), p. 159.

3. Cormac McCarthy, *The Road* (New York: Vintage Books, 2007), p. 172.

4. Plato, *The Republic,* Book 3, 414e–415c.

5. U.S. Constitution, Article I, section 9, Clause 8: "No title of nobility shall be granted by the United States: and no person holding any office of profit or trust under them, shall, without the consent of the Congress, accept of any present, emolument, office, or title, of any kind whatever, from any king, prince, or foreign state."

6. "Universal Declaration of Human Rights," General Assembly Res. 217A(III), U.N. Doc. A/810 (1948), 71. See also my "Religious Liberty and Human Dignity: A Tale of Two Declarations," *Harvard Journal of Law & Public Policy* 27 (September 22, 2003). As noted in the acknowledgments, this material previously appeared there.

7. Ibid. See also Mary Ann Glendon, "Reflections on the Universal Declaration on Human Rights," *First Things,* no. 82 (1998), p. 23: "Different

understandings of the meanings of rights usually reflect divergent concepts of man and of society, which in turn cause those who hold those understandings to have different views of reality."

8. Jacques Maritain, *Man and the State*, 4th ed. (Chicago: University of Chicago Press, 1956), p. 77.

9. "Universal Declaration of Human Rights," p. 71.

10. Ibid., p. 72.

11. Glendon, "Reflections on the Universal Declaration," p. 23.

12. Ibid., p. 24.

13. Universal Declaration of Human Rights," p. 72.

14. Mary Ann Glendon, "First of Freedoms?" *America: The National Catholic Review*, March 5, 2012, http://americamagazine.org/issue/5131/article/first-freedoms.

15. Marcello Pera, *Why We Must Call Ourselves Christians* (New York: Encounter, 2011), pp. 125–26.

Chapter Six: Thinking About Thinking About God

1. Rabbi Marc Soloway, "The God I Don't Believe In First Day Rosh Hashanah 5771," Berdichev Revival, http://www.berdichev.org/the_god_i_dont_believe.html.

2. Aristotle, *Metaphysics,* Book 12, 1072b.

3. Aristotle, *Ethics,* Book 5, Chapter 7.

4. Leo Strauss, "The Origin of the Idea of Natural Right," in *Natural Right and History* (Chicago: University of Chicago Press, 1953), p. 89.

5. Thomas Aquinas, *Summa theologica* (1264), Part 1, Question 2, Article 3.

6. "Professor Antony Flew," *Telegraph,* April 13, 2010, http://www.telegraph.co.uk/news/obituaries/culture-obituaries/books-obituaries/7586929/Professor-Antony-Flew.html.

7. Anselm of Canterbury, *Proslogion* (1078).

8. Aristotle, *Metaphysics,* Book I.

9. Tertullian, *On Prescription Against Heretics*, quoted in Étienne Gilson, *Reason and Revelation in the Middle Ages* (New York: Scribner's, 1968), p. 9.

10. Ronald W. Clark, *Einstein: The Life and Times* (New York: World, 1971), p. 414.

11. Quoted in Philip J. Davis, "A Brief Look at Mathematics and Theology," *Humanistic Mathematics Journal* (June 2002), http://www2.hmc.edu/www_common/hmnj/davis2brieflook1and2.pdf.

12. C. S. Lewis, *Mere Christianity* (New York: Macmillan, 1952), p. 31.

13. Ibid., p. 34.

14. Ibid., p. 37.

15. Ibid., p. 38.
16. Avery Dulles, "The Deist Minimum," *First Things* (January 2005), p. 8.

Chapter Seven: The Education of the Founders

1. James Walsh, *Education of the Founding Fathers of the Republic: Scholasticism in the Colonial Colleges* (New York: Fordham University Press, 1935), p. 9.
2. Frederick Rudolph, *Curriculum: A History of the American Undergraduate Course Study Since 1636* (San Francisco, CA: Jossey-Bass, 1993), pp. 26–27.
3. Theodor Hornberger, *Scientific Thought in the American Colleges, 1638–1800* (Austin: University of Texas Press, 1945), pp. 6–10.
4. Ibid., pp. 27–31.
5. Lawrence Cremlin, *American Education: The Colonial Experience* (New York: Harper, 1972), p. 512.
6. Walsh, *Education of the Founding Fathers,* p. 55.
7. Ibid., p. 8.
8. Ibid., p. 36.
9. Rudolph, *Curriculum,* p. 30.
10. George H. Nash, *Books and the Founding Fathers* (ISI Distributed Titles, 2008), p. 10.

11. Hornberger, *Scientific Thought*, p. 24.

12. Cremlin, *American Education*, p. 512.

13. René Descartes, *Meditations on First Philosophy* (1641).

14. Gottfried Leibniz, *New Essays on Human Understanding* (1709).

15. Bernard Cohen, *Science and the Founding Fathers: Science in the Political Thought of Jefferson, Franklin, Adams, and Madison* (New York: Norton, 1997), p. 20.

16. Helmut Moritz, *Science, Mind, and the Universe: An Introduction to Natural Philosophy* (Heidelberg: Wichmann, 1995), p. ix.

17. Sara Gronim, *Everyday Nature: Knowledge of the Natural World in Colonial New York* (New Brunswick, NJ: Rutgers University Press, 2007), p. 142.

18. Baden Powell, *History of Natural Philosophy from the Earliest Periods to the Present Time, Chronology of Physical and Mathematical Science* (1834; reprinted General Books, 2012), pp. xi–xvi.

19. Ibid., p. 20.

20. Nancy Pearcey and Charles Thaxton, *The Soul of Science: Christian Faith and Natural Philosophy* (Irvine, CA: Fieldstead Institute, 1994), pp. 71–72, 95.

21. Isaac Newton, *Principia: Mathematical Principles of Natural Philosophy* (1687).

22. Cohen, *Science and Founding Fathers*, p. 20.

23. Ibid.

24. John Adams to Skelton Jones, March 11, 1809, quoted in Saul K. Padover, *World of the Founding Fathers* (Gazelle, 1977), pp. 73–75.

25. Cohen, *Science and Founding Fathers*, pp. 228–30.

26. Hornberger, *Scientific Thought*, p. 25.

27. Cremlin, *American Education*, p. 513.

28. Ibid., p. 515.

29. See generally Michael Novak and Jana Novak, *Washington's God: Religion, Liberty, and the Father of Our Country* (New York: Basic Books, 2007). Cohen, *Science and Founding Fathers*, pp. 68–72.

30. Rudolph, *Curriculum*, p. 25.

31. David Barton, *Education and the Founding Fathers* (Aledo, TX: WallBuilders Press, 1993), p. 33.

32. Ibid.

33. Nash, *Books and the Founding Fathers*, p. 10.

34. Hornberger, *Scientific Thought*, p. 7.

35. Rudolph, *Curriculum*, p. 35.

Chapter Eight: Framing a Nation Under God

1. Seneca, *Deconsolationae ad Helviam* (C.E. 42), Book 8, 2–6.

2. James Madison, in *National Gazette* (March 29, 1792), emphasis in original.

3. Cicero, *De republica* (54 B.C.E.), Book 3, xxii.

4. Much of what follows originally appeared in the Becket Fund brief, *The Freedom From Religion Foundation v. Hanover School District, New Hampshire*, No. 09-2473 (1st Cir. filed April 7, 2010), http://www.becketfund.org/wp-content/uploads/2011/06/Cyrus-Response-Brief.pdf.

5. Henry of Bracton, *De Legibus et Consuetudinibus Angliæ* (1235). A variation of this phrase is carved into the pediment of Langdell Library at Harvard Law School: "NON SVB HOMINE SED SVB DEO ET LEGE."

6. Sir Edward Coke's Reports, *Prohibitions del Roy* (1607) 63, 65, emphasis added.

7. *District of Columbia v. Heller*, 554 U.S. 570, 593-94 (2008), recognizing Blackstone's work as "the preeminent authority on English law for the founding generation," quoting *Alden v. Maine*, 527 U.S. 706, 715 (1999).

8. *Alden v. Maine*, 527 U.S. 706, 715 (1999); see also, e.g., *Blakely v. Washington*, 542 U.S. 296, 313-14 (2004); *Reid v. Covert*, 354 U.S. 1, 26 (1957).

9. William Blackstone, *Commentaries on the Law of England*, 5th ed. (1773), § 2, 38–39.

10. Ibid., 41.

11. Thomas Jefferson to Henry Lee, May 8, 1825, quoted in Carl Becker, *The Declaration of Independence* (New York: Harcourt, Brace, 1922), p. 402.

12. John Locke, *Two Treatises of Government* (1690; reprint ed. Rivington, 1824), p. 246, § 195.

13. Ibid. p. 247, § 196.

14. Algernon Sidney, *Discourses Concerning Government* (1750), p. 440.

15. Thomas Jefferson, *Notes on the State of Virginia* XVIII (1781), Query XVIII.

16. George Washington, "General Orders," July 2, 1776, http://memory.loc.gov/cgi-bin/ampage?collId=mgw3&fileName=mgw3g/gwpage001.db&recNum=301, emphasis added.

17. George Washington, "General Orders," July 9, 1776, http://memory.loc.gov/cgi-bin/ampage?collId=mgw3&fileName=mgw3g/gwpage001.db&recNum=308, emphasis added.

18. James Madison, *The Debates in the Several State Conventions, on the Adoption of the Federal Constitution, as Recommended by the General Convention at Philadelphia, in 1787*, ed. Jonathan Elliot (1836), vol. 1.

19. James Madison, "Memorial and Remonstrance" (1785).

20. Thomas Jefferson, *A Bill for Establishing Religious Freedom*, June 18, 1779.

Chapter Nine: You Say Deist, I Say Theist

1. Lord Herbert of Cherbury, *De religione gentilium*, cited in John Orr, *English Deism: Its Roots and Its Fruits* (Grand Rapids, MI: Eerdmans, 1934), p. 62. See also Avery Dulles, "The Deist Minimum," *First Things* (January 2005), p. 9.

2. Ibid., p. 12.

3. Ibid., p. 13.

4. Ibid.

5. Benjamin Franklin, *The Autobiography of Benjamin Franklin* (1791), p. 1:45.

6. Ibid.

7. Quoted by James Madison, *Notes of Debates in the Federal Convention of 1787* (New York: Norton, 1987), pp. 209–10; emphasis in the original.

8. Letter to John Adams, April 11, 1823, in Thomas Jefferson and John Adams, *The Adams-Jefferson Letters*, Vol. 2, ed. Lester Cappon (North Carolina: University of North Carolina Press, 1959), p. 594.

9. Michael Novak and Jana Novak, *Washington's God: Religion, Liberty, and the Father of Our Country* (New York: Basic Books, 2007). See generally Michael Novak's pathbreaking study, *On Two Wings: Humble Faith and Common Sense at*

the American Founding, expanded ed. (New York: Encounter, 2003).

Chapter Ten: The Later Life of
a Nation Under God

1. Stephen Hawking and Leonard Mlodinow, *The Grand Design* (New York: Bantam, 2010), p. 180.
2. Ron Chernow, *Alexander Hamilton* (New York: Penguin, 2005), p. 214.
3. *Jones v. Van Zandt,* 2 McLean 597 (Ohio Cir. Ct., 1843), "Argument for the Defendant."
4. See generally Ted Widmer, "The Other Gettysburg Address," *New York Times,* November 19, 2013.
5. Abraham Lincoln, Gettysburg Address, November 19, 1863.
6. "How the Words 'Under God' Came to Be Added to the Pledge of Allegiance to the Flag," Knights of Columbus, http://www.kofc.org/un/en/resources/communications/pledgeAllegiance.pdf.
7. George M. Docherty, "One Nation Under God," February 7, 1954, 6–7, in New York Presbyterian Church Sermon Archive, http://www.nyapc.org/congregation/sermon_archives/text/1954/undergod-sermon.pdf emphasis in the original.
8. *The Pledge of Allegiance—How the Words "Under*

God" Came to Be Added to the Pledge of Allegiance to the Flag, http://www.kofc.org/un/en/resources/communications/pledgeallegiance.pdf.

9. Dwight D. Eisenhower to Luke E. Hart, Supreme Knight of the Knights of Columbus, August 17, 1954, in " 'Under God' Under Attack," in *Columbia* (September 2002), p. 9.

10. H.R. Rep. No. 83-1693 (1954), 1–2; see also S. Rep. No. 83-1287 (1954), 2.

11. H.R. Rep. No. 83-1693 (1954), 2; see also 100 Cong. Rec. 7333 (statement of Rep. Oakman [quoting William Penn]).

12. H.R. Rep. 83-1693 (1954), 2; see also 100 Cong. Rec. 7333 (statement of Rep. Oakman [quoting George Mason]).

13. Georg Brunner, "Civil Rights," in *Encyclopedia of Soviet Law,* ed. Ferdinand Joseph Maria Feldbrugge, Gerard Pieter van den Berg, and William B. Simons, 2d ed. (Dordrecht: Martinus Nijhoff, 1985), pp. 124–25.

14. 100 Cong. Rec. 7336 (1954) (statement of Rep. O'Hara).

15. Ibid., 7332 (statement of Rep. Bolton).

16. Ibid., 7333 (statement of Rep. Rabaut).

17. Ibid., 7338 (statement of Rep. Bolton).

18. Ibid., 5750 (statement of Rep. Rabaut).

19. As noted in the Acknowledgments, much of this

material previously appeared in our legal briefs in
the Pledge of Allegiance cases. See, e.g., *The
Freedom From Religion Foundation v. Hanover
School District, New Hampshire*, No. 09-2473
(1st Cir., filed April 7, 2010), Brief of Defendants-
Appellees Muriel Cyrus et al. of The Becket Fund.

20. *Newdow v. Rio Linda Union School District*,
No. 05-17257 (9th Cir., 2010), 12.

21. Ibid., 15.

Chapter Eleven: A Nation Under God

1. U.S. Constitution, Article II, section 2, Clause 2;
emphasis added.

2. Ibid., Article I, section 7, Clauses 2 and 3 also
known as the Presentment Clause.

3. Thomas Jefferson himself used *separation of church
and state* as shorthand. In his famous letter to the
Danbury Baptist Association he said, "Believing
with you that religion is a matter which lies solely
between man & his god, that he owes account to
none other for his faith or his worship, that the
legitimate powers of government reach actions only,
and not opinions, I contemplate with sovereign
reverence that act of the whole American people
which declared that their legislature should make

no law respecting an establishment of religion, or prohibiting the free exercise thereof, thus building a wall of separation between church and state." Jefferson to Nehemiah Dodge et al., January 1, 1802, http://www.loc.gov/loc/lcib/9806/danpre .html.

4. *Permoli v. Municipality no. 1 of the City of New Orleans*, 44 U.S. 589, 609 (1845). In 1833, the Supreme Court had decided *Barron v. Baltimore* in which the plaintiff, Barron, was suing the city of Baltimore, alleging that the city owed him "just compensation" under the Fifth Amendment's takings clause for having harmed his property. Chief Justice John Marshall rejected this view, arguing that the restrictions on government power contained in the Bill of Rights applied only to the federal government. "The Constitution," he wrote, "was ordained and established by the people of the United States for themselves, for their government and not for the government of the individual States," and therefore "the Fifth Amendment must be understood as restraining the power of the general government, not as applicable to the States." *Barron v. Mayor and City Council of Baltimore*, 32 U.S. 243 (1833).

5. Massachusetts Constitution (1780): "The legisla-ture shall, from time to time, authorize and require,

the several towns, parishes, precincts, and other bodies politic, or religious societies, to make suitable provision, at their own expense, for the institution of the public worship of God, and for the support and maintenance of public Protestant teachers of piety, religion and morality, in all cases where such provision shall not be made voluntary."

6. Vermont Frame of Government (1777), Section 9.
7. "A Bill for Establishing Religious Freedom," in *Thomas Jefferson: Writings*, ed. Merrill D. Peterson (New York: Library of America, 1984), pp. 347–48.
8. *Myers v. Loudoun County*, 418 F. 3d 395 (4th Cir., 2005), emphasis in original.
9. Jefferson to Madison, March 15, 1789, in *Writings*, ed. Peterson, p. 94.
10. James Madison, "Detached Memoranda" (ca. 1817), doc. 64 in Philip B. Kurland and Ralph Lerner, *The Founders' Constitution* (Chicago: University of Chicago Press, 1986).
11. See Kevin Hasson, "The Myth: Is There Religious Liberty in America?" *American Spectator* (February 2008). As noted in the Acknowledgments, this material previously appeared there.

INDEX

Self-evident, 51, 66, 92, 123,
  129, 141, 144, 175, 185
Seneca, 116, 117
Separation of church and
  state, 161, 162, 165, 166
Separation of powers, 162,
  163, 164, 165
Shiva (Hindu god), 10
Sidney, Algernon, 124, 125
Slavery, 55, 147, 148
  Slaves, 56, 147
Slip Hill Grade School, West
  Virginia, 27
Small, William, 112
Society, 115
Society of the Sons of the
  American Revolution,
  The, 151
Socrates, 83
Somebody, 95
Something, 94, 95
  Cosmic Something, 99
  Something-ists, 18, 94
Son of God, 88
Soviet legal theory, 157
Soviet Russia, 152
  Soviet, 160
  Soviets, 153, 155
Spanish Inquisition, 59
Spinoza, Baruch, 113
Stalin, 50
State, 46, 57, 106, 160
States (American), 53, 170
Stone, Justice Harlan F., 28
Strauss, Leo, 83

Supreme Being, 18, 57, 67,
  99, 105, 114, 122, 138
  Being, 110, 186
  Fountain of Justice, 54
  Patron of Order, 54
Supreme Council, 154
Supreme Court of the United
  States, 3, 4, 15, 16, 19,
  21, 25, 28, 29, 30, 31, 32,
  35, 43, 45, 57, 121, 167,
  171, 172, 174, 176, 181,
  182
  Supreme Court Justices, 15,
  28, 29, 173, 174
"Supremely perfect being,"
  108
System of checks and
  balances, 162

Tar and feathers, 34
  Tarred and feathered, 26, 38
Telos, 82
Tenth Amendment, 52, 53
Tenth Circuit Court of
  Appeals in Denver, 39
Tertullian, 90
Theism, 50, 60, 76, 132,
  140, 141
  Theist, 98, 146
  Theists, 98, 141
Theocracy, 17, 55, 189
Theology, 87, 89, 92, 93, 94,
  105, 122, 137, 141, 188
Theoretical physics, 109
Thomson, W., 109

U.S. Court of Appeals for the
Ninth Circuit (San
Francisco), 6, 42, 43, 44,
45, 158, 174
U.S. Senate, 42, 163, 164
United Nations, 68, 70
UN Charter, 70
UN General Assembly, 69
Un-American, 166
Unalienable Rights, 58, 123,
158, 175
UNESCO Committee on the
Theoretical Bases of
Human Rights (1947), 68
(*see also* Philosopher's
Committee)
United States of America,
153
United States, 23, 26, 53,
58, 73, 146, 152, 164,
169
Universal Declaration of
Human Rights (1948),
69, 70, 71, 74
Unmoved Mover, 98, 107,
140

Van Zandt, John, 147
Vasudeva, 15
Vermont, 168, 171

Veto Clause, 164
Virgil, 103
Virginia, 168, 170, 172, 180
Virginia's constitution, 180
Virginia Bill for
Establishing Religious
Freedom, 128
Virginia Declaration of
Rights, 180
Virginia legislature, 179,
180

Washington, D.C., 150
Washington, George
(president, general), 53,
54, 105, 112, 126, 140,
150, 160
West Virginia, 27, 37
*West Virginia State Board of
Education v. Barnette,*
31, 32, 38, 176
William and Mary, 102,
112
Winthrop, John, 112
World War II, 37
Wyoming, 26

Yale, 102
Yale Law School, 15
Yitzhak, Reb Levi, 79

A NOTE ON THE TYPE

This book was set in Sabon, a typeface designed by Jan Tschichold in 1964. It was named for a sixteenth-century type-founder, Jakob Sabon, a student of Claude Garamond. The typeface is a modern revival of a type issued by the Egenolff-Berner foundry in 1592, based on roman characters of Claude Garamond and italic characters of Robert Granjon.